"GIRLS, YOU
JUST DON'T GET IT!"

Also by Jennifer Austin Leigh

A Little Book of Listening Skills:
A Collection of Essential Practices for Conveying Genuine Love and Respect
(coauthored with Mark Brady, PhD)

"GIRLS, YOU JUST DON'T GET IT!"

WHAT GUYS WANT YOU TO KNOW ABOUT LOVE AND RESPECT.

By

Jennifer Austin Leigh, PsyD

IGNITE REALITY
Aspen, Colorado
San Fransico, California

Ignite Reality LLC
Dr. Jennifer Austin Leigh
237 Kearny St. #201
San Francisco, CA 94108

Leigh, Jennifer, PysD
Girls, You Just Don't Get It!

ISBN 978-0-9816258-2-9

10 09 08 07 06
5 4 3 2 1

Book Design by Colin O'Brien - www.studiotaraz.com
Back cover photo by Michael Morrissey
Hair styled by Amee Wong, Vidal Sassoon, San Francisco

Printed in the United States

To my mother and father, Helen and Doyle,
for patiently waiting for me to polish my Dream Girl crown.
And to every teen girl who struggles to love, cherish and accept herself.

CONTENTS

ACKNOWLEDGMENTS

I could not have written this book without the help of:

My children, John, Natalie, Louis, and William, who graciously allowed me to go into the trenches with them and learn what was going on in teens' lives.

The thousands of wonderful friends I have on MySpace, who sent me letters, asked questions and took the time to be interviewed. Your support and encouragement to write a book you needed helped me burn the midnight oil.

Thank you to:

Winnie, for her keen eye, unfaltering friendship, and lessons in dying with ... dignity. Bruce, who constantly breathed wind beneath my wings and listened to hundreds of conversations about the book without interrupting. Mark, who taught me "healing wanting to happen" and kept me up to date on neuroscience research—his concern for my limbic system helped me keep writing when the going got tough. Sarah, for her help above and beyond the call of duty—I could not function without her organizational skills and retail therapy outings.

DISCLAIMER

I interviewed hundreds of guys and girls from twenty-three different countries for this book. Interviews were held in person, over the phone, and through the Internet.

All of the stories in this book are factual; in some cases, the stories were drawn from composites of teens I have worked with, due to similarities in their responses. For reasons of privacy and confidentiality, only first names (and in some cases, the name of the person's country of origin) have been included. When requested, the name was either changed or listed as anonymous.

I have done my best to use direct quotes and attribute them correctly with the appropriate names. If I have made any mistakes in representing what was shared with me or attributed a quote to the wrong person, it was not intentional.

I greatly appreciate all of the time that people took to answer the surveys, as well as to respond to blogs and bulletins on MySpace.

"A lady is a woman who makes a man behave like a gentleman."
–Russell Lynes

intro

Girls, Start Here

When I created my MySpace page, I was amazed how many guys wrote, "Dear Dr. Jenn, girls just don't get it. They don't seem to understand the importance of love and respect anymore." So, I interviewed hundreds of guys from all over the world and asked exactly what they wish girls knew. Some of the secrets guys shared were so surprising, I had to write this book and share them with you.

If you are like most girls, you probably think that guys want you to be a super hot, sexy, boobalicous babe who knows how to tease and please in order to win a guys heart. That's what the media certainly tells you. But it's not what guys told me.

You may also think that drama queens and cruel girls rule, while nice, kind girls are so not cool. But that's not what guy's think.

Guys want you to get that the key to winning love and respect is to have love and respect for yourself first. Guys know if you start there, you can then give love and respect to guys. And that's what they want; your love and respect. Just like that's what you want from them.

This book isn't about changing who you are to make a guy happy. The goal isn't to put a guy on a pedestal. The goal, girls, is to put yourself on a pedestal. Not all snooty-like of course, but in a way that helps you make decisions that ultimately create more happiness, harmony and health for yourself and others.

Guys want you to be proud, confident, kind and respectful of yourself and others. They want you to be the girl worth loving and respecting: a Dream Girl. Guys don't want you to end up a just-in-his-jeans girl; the girl that guys think are only worth a meaningless sexual encounter.

Start here. Think of respect as the crown that every Dream Girl wears. All the secrets you are about to learn are the many jewels in that crown. It's a confusing world out there, with way too many jolts that can knock the jewels from your Dream Girl crown. If you should trip or stumble along the way to getting love and respect, don't worry. Just pick yourself up, adjust your crown, and keep on walking. Hold your head up high and stay focused on the love and respect you deserve. Don't give up. Ever.

It's All About Respect

"A hot chick pulled up beside me in a parking lot yesterday in a new BMW! It was love at first sight. I thought it was my lucky day! I couldn't wait to see what the rest of her looked like when she got out of the car. She got out of the car wearing tight booty shorts and a see-through tank top with no bra. She answered her cell phone and started bitching out someone. I immediately lost interest in getting to know her. She may have been good for a tap, but any girl who doesn't have enough self-respect to dress better than a hoochie momma and [who] bitches out her friends isn't going to win my heart. I turned and walked away."
—John, USA

They say first impressions are everything. That's certainly true in today's world, especially when it comes to relationships. Whether you realize it or not, girls, every guy makes a decision about you from the moment he meets you (or in John's case, the moment just before he almost meets you). They want to know if you are worth getting to know, someone to potentially care about and respect, or if you're more likely to be worth only a meaningless sexual encounter.

John, the young man quoted above, instinctively knew that the hot babe who pulled up in the new car was not a Dream Girl. Why? She didn't appear to have much self-respect or respect for others by the way she dresssed or by how she spoke. The girls that guys respect and care about understand that respect is the cornerstone of a loving relationship. Dream Girls know that to get respect, they must give it—not only to others, but to themselves. It all starts with you.

Respect can be a challenge, especially in today's world. In this chapter, you will discover crucial information about respect: how to get it and how to give it. You'll learn how things that happened to you when you were growing up may have an impact on the level of self-respect you have. There will even be a quiz you can take that will immediately show you the impact of your "growing-up wounds," as well as give you some ideas as to how to move beyond your wounds.

You will also learn how to silence your Itty Bitty Shitty Committee— the collection of negative thoughts residing in your head that can wreak havoc with your self-respect. By learning all you can about respect, you will be well on your way to becoming a Dream Girl and avoid the heartache of being a just-in-his-jeans girl.

what guys want you to know:

Guys like girls with self-respect. Knowing that is the first step on the road to becoming a Dream Girl.

Secret No. 1

WHAT IS RESPECT?

What is that magical quality some special girls have that draws guys to them and keeps them there with seemingly little effort? Most girls think it has something to do with dressing sexy, being flirtatious, or turning the spotlight on themselves so that they can show off and get a guy's attention. Actually, it has very little to do with any of those things.

Although being sexy or flirtatious certainly gets you noticed, it doesn't make a guy stick around. True attraction that lasts beyond the stirrings of sexual attraction is built on one important factor: respect.

Respect has many close attributes to love. Respect for others means you have a high regard for people, you trust them, and you never intend them any harm. Respect for yourself—or self-respect—means just that: you have a high regard for yourself. It doesn't mean you can walk around all snooty, thinking you're better than everyone else—not even close. It does mean, however, that you know who you are and, just as importantly, who you're not, and that you're perfectly okay with that. You know deep down that you don't need to impress anyone but yourself and that self-confidence commands respect.

A girl with self-respect is a girl who likes herself, takes herself seriously, and has good values she'll stick to, even in the face of peer pressure. And because she has good values, she's also a girl who knows how to trust her instincts. That means she knows what's right for her is not necessarily what the media says is right, or what her friends or parents say, but what she knows inside herself to be true. Take a look:

(((What Guys Are Saying About Girls with Self-Respect

I know a girl has self-respect when she says "no" and doesn't give in to doing something she doesn't want to do. That's a big turn-on for guys.
—Ezra, USA

I like a girl with self-respect because I never have to feel like I am just a placeholder, filling her need to have a boyfriend so she can feel good about it.
—Josh, USA

You know a girl has self-respect when she is nice and treats others right.
—Nicholas, USA

Girls who have self-respect are adored by guys, because guys know that girls who have a lot of self-respect will usually show them respect as well.

I asked hundreds of guys ages fourteen to twenty-one from twenty-three countries to complete this statement: "I respect girls who _____." Most of them answered by saying "respect themselves" or "respect me." Clearly, respect is highly valued.

WHERE IT ALL STARTS

Respect is essential to becoming a Dream Girl. Why? The answer goes back to an old saying: "You can't love someone unless you love yourself." The same is true about respect.

Unless you know how to offer compassion and kindness to yourself, you'll never know what it means to offer compassion and kindness to another human being. And love and respect are about compassion and kindness, among many other things.

A girl who doesn't respect herself—let alone other people—is not a Dream Girl. How could she be? If she can't respect herself, it's highly doubtful that she will respect others. Girls with little respect for others almost guarantee that they will be seen as just-in-his-jeans girls.

WHY IT'S HARD—BUT NOT IMPOSSIBLE—TO DEVELOP SELF-RESPECT

Self-respect can be hard to achieve, especially in today's world. In just a few short years, the communications revolution has changed the way we view sex, violence, and women. The invention of the Internet changed the scope of our world and allowed anyone and everyone with an opinion and a computer to have an impact on our culture. The advent of cell phones, video games, virtual social networks, hip-hop, high-speed communication, and "instant everything" brings us to an age where miscommunication is rampant and women are objectified, devalued, and ultimately disrespected more than ever.

With all that's going on out there, it's harder and harder for girls today to achieve self-respect. I mean, think of all the roadblocks you have to overcome.

For one, there's the media—or, I should say, the way the media depicts women.

If you believe the images you see in magazine ads, TV commercials, and the movies, you would think the only way a girl can be accepted or respected is if she's bone thin with big breasts, a sassy haircut, a flawless complexion, and not one little teeny tiny bump of cellulite on her thighs or bootylicious butt. But how many girls in the real world look like that? Usually only girls who starve themselves or spend their lives at the gym actually have supermodel or celebrity bodies. Think about it. Along with severe diets and long workouts, a lot of the "beautiful people" you see in the media have undergone some sort of surgery to assist them in their appearance.

Then there are all those music videos, where girls in bikinis or lingerie either grind their hot little bodies up against whichever guy is pawing them, twirl themselves around a pole like a stripper, lounge around the pool or bed with their legs spread, or simply stand around doing nothing like they're a live-

> **DR. JENN SAYS...**
>
> *The media doesn't have your best interest at heart. Don't believe everything you read or see.*

action play toy. Not to mention the lyrics in these songs, which commonly refer to girls as "bitches" and "hos," whose only purpose in life is to sexually please a man. On top of all that, there are popular video games like *Grand Theft Auto III*, where players can score extra points for having sex with a girl, and even *more* points for killing her afterward! Not only is this so not cool, it sends a very bad message to guys and girls alike.

The checkout line in the grocery store, convenience stores, and scores of other retail outlets are also some of the worst places for a want-to-be Dream Girl. Why? Read the headlines on some of the top-selling magazines: "How to Make Him Sizzle This Summer," "The Top Ways to Tease and Please Him," and "Let Your Freak in the Sheets Flag Fly!" Before you can even buy your food, shampoo, or tampons, you are barraged by messages screaming at you that the way to a guy's heart is just through his zipper. That can't feel good in your heart and soul.

The fashion world also makes it hard for girls today to feel good about themselves, what with suggestive designs for lower-and-lower-cut jeans and smaller and smaller tops that show more and more cleavage and belly. These fashions are bad enough for grown women to deal with, but for girls your age and younger, this trend toward showing more and more skin makes it harder for a Dream Girl to know what look really shows off her best asset; her self-respect.

Then there's the whole YouTube/viral video phenomenon, where you can not only create your own video but post it right away for the entire world to see with just a few clicks of the mouse. And while that's kinda cool—hey, we all like to visit YouTube and other sites like that, and we all like to share videos with our friends—it also compounds the problem.

Sure, I know that when you get down to it, most of the stuff we see on YouTube is either silly or kinda stupid. But I know, and you know, that a lot of it isn't. Many of these images perpetuate not only the media's idea of the "perfect girl," but also the less-than-perfect antics of the drunken teens on videos like *Girls Gone Wild*, where a momentary lapse in judgment (like flashing your boobies in front of a live camera) is captured on tape, conceivably forever, for all the world to see. Not only do some people take this stuff seriously, but with today's technology—where you can instant-message a video through your laptop, cell phone, Sidekick, BlackBerry, or iPhone faster than you can think or blink—these images are being rapidly spread to a potentially massive audience in more ways than you ever imagined.

Finally, there are pornographic Web sites that feature videos of blood and gore alongside some of the most debased images of women ever created. While some of these places are pay sites, many of them are free, which means that children and teenagers can access these images with just a click of the mouse. Since curiosity can get even the best of people, chances are that a lot of people your age have probably visited these sites at least once, if only to grab a peek.

Put all these obstacles together, and it's not a pretty picture. No wonder so many girls today are stumbling on the path to becoming a Dream Girl. Why worry about a little thing like self-respect when you're bombarded with media images and messages that practically encourage you to throw your self-respect out the window?

We live in a world of not just mass media but *fast* media. Did you know that by the time you turn twenty-one, you will have already seen over twenty-three million advertisements? That's more ads than some of your moms have seen in their entire lifetimes. And you know something? The big corporations who make those ads and create those music videos and video games spend billions of dollars every year on marketing campaigns designed to convince you that the only way to a guy's heart is through your body—even though they know full well that's totally wack.

Companies know that, deep down, a girl's biggest assets are her heart, her compassion, and her ability to love and listen. But they can't sell you any of that, because they know those are things you *already have*. And even if you may have nodded off a few times in economics class, you know that companies are in business to (1) sell products and (2) make people think they need to have the products these companies sell. It all comes to down to money. And since these companies can't sell you something you already have, they make you think you need something else—namely, their product. So they spend all that money creating all those images to make you think that the only way to attract a guy is to act like the latest celebrity who is always making headlines with her wild adventures, and to dress like any of the come-and-get-me pixies you see in the pages of some magazines or the latest Abercrombie & Fitch catalog. They want you to flash your boobies like the wild girls on spring break or behave like some lobotomized sex kitten because, after all, that's what guys want, right?

Wrong.

Talk about degrading. Not only does that disrespect you, it disrespects guys, too. It makes you think that guys today are so shallow they don't care about things like self-respect and your ability to respect them; all they want from a girl is for someone to rock their world. And while there are some guys who are like that (hey, I dated a few myself, and I'm sure you have, too), if you stop and ask most guys what they're really looking for in a girl, you find that what the media message "what guys really want" is not what they want at all. Guys are not happy with the way the media portrays women. Listen in:

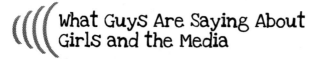

What Guys Are Saying About Girls and the Media

I love women. It makes me angry how the world has perverted women—and sex, for that matter. The words hos and bitches are completely disrespectful remarks about women.
—Jason, New Zealand

The negative remarks about women make me want to knock out the person who has said them.
—Gary, Ireland

The words hos, bitches, sluts, etc. are used so much I don't think most people even know they are using them anymore.
—Kay, South Africa

The hip-hop rap culture is all negative to women. The women who appear as rump shakers in music videos (as well as strippers and porn stars) are women who need or want money so badly, they do work that reduces the value of their gender in our society. Girls growing up today see that stuff on TV, and when they hear their peers using the same debasing language, they get the idea that rap videos are the way the world really is. They come away thinking that the best they can do is be a "fly bitch."
—Joshua, USA

PARK YOURSELF IN NEUTRAL AND BANISH YOUR IBSC

As hurtful as media stereotypes can be, they're not the only things that can prevent a girl from achieving self-respect. Everyone has an inner collection of negative thoughts—what I like to call an IBSC, or *Itty Bitty Shitty Committee*—that can make us feel ... well, you know what

I'm saying. We not only listen to these messages far more than we do to positive self-messages, we tend to add even more negative thoughts to this collection as we grow up.

Perhaps you hear your father's voice telling you that you'll "never amount to anything." Maybe you remember the time your mother called you "stupid" or the teacher who embarrassed you before the entire class by saying, "How can you be so lazy?" Or maybe they're just mental hang-overs from your last Private Pity Party: "Nobody loves me." "Everybody hates me." "Why don't I have a boyfriend?" "Why can't I do anything right?" "I wish I was thinner." "I wish I was taller." "I wish I didn't have to wear this stupid retainer."

It doesn't matter what those messages are, who said them, or how they got into your system. What matters is that *they're still in your system*, enjoying rent-free space in your brain; and the more you think about them, the more you give voice to them, the longer you keep them alive.

Even Dream Girls have their moments of self-doubt. What makes them different from a just-in-his-jeans girl—or anyone else who doesn't have a positive self-image—is that they know what it takes to keep their Itty Bitty Shitty Committee from having complete sway over their lives. And the amazing thing is, in many cases, just being aware of what your IBSC is and what it's telling you is the first step in teaching yourself how to shut it off permanently.

What about you? What are some negative messages you tell yourself? Can you think of at least five? List them below and on the following page.

Memo to Me:
Get rid of the following IBSC messages

 *Memo to Me cont.*

Okay, now that you've jotted them down, here's how to keep those itty bitty shitty messages from controlling the rest of your life.

Imagine you're at the Cineplex. There's nobody else in the theater; it's just you and you alone watching the movie play in front of you on the big screen. You've kicked back; you're totally focused, following the story, taking it all in. You're not judging whether the movie is good or bad; you're just sitting there in total neutral mode, simply *observing*, enjoying the movie.

Feels good, doesn't it? There's absolutely no pressure. It's a nice mini vacation from all your thoughts and worries.

On your way home from the movie, you're back in the real world; and suddenly, one of your Itty Bitty Shitty Committee thoughts creeps in.

Instead of letting that negative thought spread through you like a virus, go into what I call "movie mode." You'll be doing just what you were doing in the theater, only the "movie" you are going to be watching is *you*—or, I should say, you having your Itty Bitty Shitty Committee thought. Say to yourself, "Here I go again, having this Itty Bitty Shitty Committee thought." Make sure you watch yourself with no judgments or emotions. You must be a neutral observer. You can't get mad at yourself or berate yourself for having the thought. The simple act of neutrally observing yourself having the negative thought will begin to silence the thought. I'll explain why in just a moment.

We all have moments of self-doubt, starting in childhood and continuing through adulthood. That's one of those things on our road through life that everyone has to deal with. But that doesn't mean we have to let those moments of self-doubt block our path to self-respect.

The more mindful you are of the presence of these negative thoughts, the more aware you'll become of the power you give them. The more aware you are of the power you give them, the better you'll be at silencing those thoughts and putting your focus on more positive, productive things.

You can't strong-arm your IBSC. Why? When you think about it, your IBSC is just like a bunch of itty bitty bullies. What's the best way get rid of bullies? That's right, you ignore them. If you don't play their game, they lose interest and leave you alone.

Your IBSC is no different. The next time they try to mess with your head, go into movie mode. When you don't give them any energy, they go away. That's why movie mode works.

That's what my friend Sarah did. Sarah's an eighteen-year-old Dream-Girl-in-training who had a really hard time dealing with her Itty Bitty Shitty Committee—especially when it came to feeling like she wasn't worthy enough of a guy's attention—until she learned how to go into movie mode. Whenever she found herself dragged down by negative thoughts, she simply went about her business and "watched" herself having the thought. "Here I am having that same old thought, here I am thinking I don't deserve to be loved or respected," she would say, sometimes even out loud when she was alone. She didn't get upset or angry with herself. She just parked herself in neutral and went into movie mode until the thoughts simply didn't have as much emotional punch, and she was able to let them go.

> **DR. JENN SAYS...**
>
> *I silenced a lot of my Itty Bitty Shitty Committee thoughts using movie mode. You can, too!*

what guys want you to know:

It's really hard if your negative self-thoughts overrule anything nice that we have to say about you.

Secret No. 2

We spend a lot of time in our lives worrying about a lot of different things. Now, some things we absolutely should worry about, like how we hurt our friend's feelings last week when we said something we really didn't mean in anger. All you can do is apologize and hope your friend forgives you. But some of the other things we worry about are not worth dwelling on at all. A good rule of thumb is, if you can't go back and say you're sorry or fix something, stop worrying about it! Learn to let it go.

Yes, your school probably would have won the girls' state basketball championship last year had you not missed those two free throws with your team down by one point and only one second left in the game. Yes, it sucked at the time, and it still sucks to think about it now. But that's all in the past, right? You can't do anything to change what happened, no matter how hard you try, so why let it ruin the rest of your life?

Why not think about the positive aspects of the experience, like how all of your teammates consoled you after the final buzzer sounded, or how hard you all worked to get yourselves in position to play in the championship game in the first place, and use that as a stepping stone for moving forward?

When you look at it that way, that itty bitty negative becomes ittier and bittier ... while your ability to respect yourself continues to grow.

That's what happened with Sarah. The more she taught herself to go into movie mode whenever negative thoughts crept in, the quieter her Itty Bitty Shitty Committee became. With time, she was able to replace the negative energy about herself with more love and positive energy.

That positive energy began to show in the way she carried herself and how she treated others. And talk about a snowball effect: the more Sarah came to like and respect herself, the more attractive she became to others, as a friend to girls and as a potential girlfriend to guys.

Guys want you to learn to silence your Itty Bitty Shitty Committee. See for yourself:

What Guys Are Saying About Girls Itty Bitty Shitty Committees

I want girls to stop being so hard on themselves, like calling themselves fat or ugly. Guys don't like that, especially when it gets excessive.
　　—Erik, USA

Stop worrying about how you look or how big you think you look. If a guy is interested in you, he probably loves the way you look.
　　—Brian, USA

Stop talking down about yourselves. It's an incredible turnoff! It puts guys in a bad spot. What are we supposed to say to you? It's really hard if you can't take a compliment and your negative self-thoughts overrule anything nice that I may have to say about you.
　　—Russell, USA

RESPECT MEANS TO LOOK AGAIN

You are one of a kind out of six billion people (give or take a handful). Not only is that cool, that's downright miraculous. What that means is, no matter what anyone tries to tell you, you are indeed a very special person. *Nothing* and *no one* can take that away from you. Not your classmates. Not your teacher. Not your parents. Not your Itty Bitty Shitty Committee.

The word "respect" comes from the Latin word *respectus*, meaning the act of looking back at one's self, or literally to "look again." If you were to look back at yourself, beyond all the flaws you think you have, beyond what all the voices your IBSC tells you, what do you see? What is deep down inside of you? Look back, over and over and over again, until you can see who you really are, until you see the unique, wonderful you. This is what people mean when they say it's what's inside that counts.

Then once you've looked back at yourself, look again at all the people who have come into your life and may have made you feel bad, even the teacher who embarrassed you, even the "friends" who may have hurt you or dissed you for reasons you don't understand. Can you see beyond their flaws?

Believe me; I know how hard that can be sometimes. But promise me—and promise yourself—that you'll take the high road of looking again at people and do your best to look past their faults and past your hurt feelings and move on. Respect the fact *that they are just as unique as you are,* just as different, and I promise you that you'll be the better for it.

> **DR. JENN SAYS...**
>
> *Taking the high road to see beyond people's flaws attracts love and respect.*

When you look for the best in others, you'll also find it in yourself. That's what positive, successful, well-rounded people do. That's what Dream Girls do, too.

HURT HAPPENS IN ALL SHAPES AND SIZES

Each individual person may be a unique miracle, and that's a beautiful thing. If only everyone were perfect. Unfortunately, and as we know all too well, that's often not the case.

Human beings have an ugly side. Human beings are capable of saying things or doing things that are downright mean and cruel. Getting our feelings hurt and our egos bashed by others happens to everyone, from the time we are children playing on the playground right on through our lives as adults.

In other words, hurt happens. Sometimes people hurt us deliberately, while other times they end up hurting us when that's the furthest thing from their mind. But they hurt us just the same. And yes, sometimes those moments can be really painful, but it's all part of growing up.

If you were mistreated growing up or had a traumatic experience, those moments can often leave you with deep emotional scars that can impact the rest of your life. Even something as seemingly harmless as a nasty text message from someone can follow you around like an endless loop playing in your head and influence the way you feel about yourself and others.

Everyone's threshold for hurt is different, and what causes you to hurt may not cause someone else to hurt. But when the hurt is bad enough, it can literally change your brain structure.

The limbic system is the part of the brain responsible for survival. Whenever you feel threatened or hurt, your limbic system fires up and causes to you to fight, flee, or freeze. One theory about the brain is that when you feel you can't defend yourself, your limbic system "tells" some neurons in your brain to go a bit haywire, and, as a result, they keep firing when they should have stopped. When you look at a certain type of brain scan, there are "holes" in the brain of people who have had a lot of trauma.

Let's say your grandfather beat you when you were growing up. If you couldn't defend yourself, chances are neurons in your brain kept firing. A special kind of neuron—kind of like a paramedic neuron—rushed in and wrapped itself around the out of control ones. The "paramedic neurons" kept the neurons that were out of control locked down. Now you have a part of your brain that doesn't work properly. It is no longer connected to the whole brain circuitry, which means that the locked-down neurons keep you from being able to access your prefrontal cortex, the part of your brain that helps you make rational, logical, life and love affirming decisions

So, if your grandfather beat you, and you couldn't defend yourself, a small area of your brain got locked down and you now have fewer connections to the logical decision-making area of your brain. And guess what? Your ability to respect yourself, like your ability to shut down your IBSC by going into movie mode, is often based on how able you are to make logical, rational decisions.

Your body, like everything else in nature, has a built-in desire to heal itself. If you fall and skin your knee, the cells in your body will automatically generate new cells so that the cut on your knee will eventually heal. Your brain is no different than any other part of your body when it comes to dealing with pain. Despite what happened with your grandfather and how his abuse "locked down" or "hurt" your brain, your brain wants to heal itself.

Now here's the tricky part that can derail you from becoming a Dream Girl. Your brain wants to heal, but its healing process is not as straightforward as your scraped knee healing itself. Your brain looks for ways to recreate the old wound so that the next time the hurt happens, the brain "gets it right," meaning, you can defend yourself and unlock the neurons that were previously shut down.

Using the abusive grandfather as an example, let's say that in your efforts to heal the scars he left you, you either consciously or unconsciously create a new situation similar to the one that locked down your brain in the first place. You may, for example, date a guy who beats you. Instead of calling the authorities and cutting all ties with him, you decide to stick around and try to win his love; deep down, you want to overcome the pain your grandfather inflicted on you as a child. As noble as having the will to conquer your past hurt sounds, the problem with that scenario is that it will only cause you more pain, both physical and mental. Staying in an abusive relationship will not unlock the part of your brain that is wounded. Your body, heart, mind, soul, and spirit all pay the price. So does your self-respect.

Recreating old wounds in an attempt to heal puts girls at risk of becoming just-in-his-jeans girls. Here's what Alice discovered about her old wounds. Alice grew up with a father who was emotionally cold and distant. He was often gone, and, when he was home, he was rude, sarcastic, and downright verbally abusive at times. Alice put up with it as best as she could, but sometimes she swore back at her dad when he went off on her.

When Alice turned eighteen, she met a guy she absolutely flipped over. She had to be with him all the time. But he was emotionally distant, and, when he got angry with her, he swore at her. At first, Alice was shocked by his outbursts, but it didn't take long until she was swearing back at him. Alice found herself angry most of the time, and their swear-fests turned into door slamming, nasty text messages, and put-downs on Facebook. They were angry with each other more than they were happy with each other.

One day, Alice told me that she realized she was actually recreating her relationship with her father by seeing this particular guy. She had no way to heal the relationship with her dad, but she was trying to master it via her new boyfriend. She had subconsciously picked a guy who would help her recreate her old wounds. Alice finally understood that she wasn't going to heal her old wounds this way, and all she was doing was feeding the behaviors that work against her becoming a Dream Girl. No one wants to hang around a girl who is so angry that she swears all the time and allows guys to mistreat her.

Alice wanted to heal, but there was just reenactment without resolution. Don't despair. There are ways you can heal your brain. We'll get to that soon. Just being aware that you have locked-down neurons because you have been wounded and that your brain is looking for ways to heal is a step toward healing. Understanding how your brain works helps you understand why you behave the way you do. Alice understood why she was in the relationship and chose to get out of it before more damage was done.

You don't have to be the victim of blatant abuse to have a negative effect on your brain. John Bowlby (1907–1990), a very smart but also very controversial psychoanalyst from Great Britain, understood that other events harmed our brains. He put forth the "theory of attachment." Bowlby discovered that children need good, solid, loving attachment to their parents or caregivers in order for their brains to grow properly. This means that, if one of your parents abandoned you in some way, even if they didn't want to or mean to (perhaps through divorce or separation or simply by working long hours), it may have wounded your brain.

Remember that when you are wounded, you are operating from a place of fear and pain. It's highly doubtful that you are being self-respectful or respectful to the person with whom you are recreating the old wound. Being part of a relationship that fosters disrespect hurts your chances of wearing that sparkling Dream Girl crown.

THE GROWING-UP WOUNDS QUIZ

Growing-up wounds are not unlike the negative thoughts in your IBSC. That being the case, it shouldn't surprise you to know that the best way to deal with them is to first become aware of them. Here is a quiz you can take to discover some of the things that possibly made a negative impact on your brain.

How to take this quiz:

1. First, put a check next to anything you have experienced.
2. Then, once you've gone through the entire list, go back to the top and take the quiz again. Only this time, put an R next to anything that happened to you repeatedly.
3. Finally, once you've finished repeating the quiz, go back and take it a third time. This time, put a T next to anything that caused you to feel traumatized in any way. A good rule of thumb is that if you felt like you wanted to fight, or run away or you froze, you felt trauma.

THE QUIZ

- ❑ _ _ Physical, sexual, verbal or emotional abuse
- ❑ _ _ Disrespectful treatment (e.g., insults, lies)
- ❑ _ _ Harsh discipline, like being hit, or demeaned
- ❑ _ _ Valued for achievements, not for who you are
- ❑ _ _ Unreasonably high adult expectations of you
- ❑ _ _ Ignoring or rejection of your painful emotions by parents or caretakers
- ❑ _ _ Love or attention based on your good behavior
- ❑ _ _ Racism, sexism
- ❑ _ _ Over control by caretakers such as not giving you proper autonomy

❑ __ __ Physical or emotional neglect

❑ __ __ Insufficient nurturing contact, holding, or nonsexual touch

❑ __ __ Lack of opportunities to form attachments

❑ __ __ Lack of stimulation

❑ __ __ Lack of autonomy (meaning, lack of sense of self)

❑ __ __ Unfulfilled promises

❑ __ __ Lack of communication

❑ __ __ Left out of school activities

❑ __ __ Important events unacknowledged

❑ __ __ Messages being ignored or purposely not being returned

❑ __ __ MySpace or Facebook hostilities

❑ __ __ Hurtful gossip about you

❑ __ __ Illnesses, injuries, medical procedures, or surgeries

❑ __ __ Subjected to general anesthesia or IV sedation

❑ __ __ Loss of attachments (separation or death)

❑ __ __ Being abandoned

❑ __ __ Given up for adoption

❑ __ __ Overstimulation/overly stressed

❑ __ __ Developmental frustrations and fears

❑ __ __ Inescapable restraints

❑ __ __ Major changes (e.g., new sibling, home, or school)

❑ __ __ Primary caretaker dysfunction (e.g., anxiety, grief, anger, illness)

❑ __ __ Parent/guardian disputes, separation or divorce

❑ __ __ Primary caretaker alcoholism or drug abuse

❑ __ __ Dysfunctional family

❑ __ __ Natural disasters (e.g., fires, floods, earthquakes, tornadoes, hurricanes)

❑ __ __ Exposure to violence (through real life or the media)

❑ __ __ Other frightening events

❑ __ __ Disappointments or unforeseen negative occurrences

❑ __ __ Arguments with caretakers, peers, or siblings

❑ __ __ Being dumped or broken up via e-mail or text

❑ __ __ Bullied

❑ __ __ Prenatal or birth trauma

❏ __ __   Any other experience not listed above, but which has also caused you great emotional or physical pain (write them below):

_____

_____

_____

_____

_____

_____

_____

(Adapted from *Tears and Tantrums* by Aletha J. Solter, Shining Star Press, 1998 and from *A Little Book of Listening Skills* by Mark Brady, PhD, and Jennifer Austin Leigh, PsyD, Paiedia Press, 2005.)

"Be kind to everyone you meet for we are all fighting a hard battle." This quote is often attributed to Plato, the Greek philosopher (424/423 BC to 384/347 BC), or to Philo of Alexandria (AD 20 to 50). Whichever man said it, it is a wonderful reminder that every one of us has battle scars or baggage or issues or however else we choose to describe our wounds from the past. There's not much we can do about that; it's part of the human experience. Yet, if we're not careful, the wounds of our past can prevent us from seeing ourselves or others in a loving, compassionate way. That's why it's important to know your past history of hurts. Look over the quiz and see how many things have an *R* or a *T* by them. Those things had the biggest impact on you.

> **DR. JENN SAYS...**
>
> *Be kind to yourself and others. We are all wounded, wanting to heal.*

When you have growing-up wounds or the blues (and we all do), sometimes it feels the only way to deal with them is to numb them with booze, drugs, sex, or to engage in harmful practices like anorexia, bulimia, or self-mutilation. None of these are behaviors are healthy; nor do they put you in the bull's-eye of being a Dream Girl. Sadly, they do just the opposite.

Dream Girls may want to numb out, but they learn to become brave enough to reach out for help. That's what makes them Dream Girls. They face their pains and fears and find healthy ways to heal.

HOW TO BEGIN HEALING

Healing old wounds takes time and effort. Some people need to seek therapeutic help, and others do fine working on their past pains on their own. Not sure where to start? You can always talk to a trusted adult if you need help making a decision about how to get the help you need. Here are three ideas for healing yourself that are amazingly effective. As a side benefit, each of these practices can help you heal your brain. And they also help you grow new neurons, which is a wonderful thing.

One way to deal with your growing-up wounds is to just go out and play—you know, the kind of play where you use your imagination and have fun in the process. Hey, kids aren't the only ones who need time to play. Everyone needs to make room in their lives for pure, unfiltered fun—even adults, even you. Play is not only a good dose of medicine for what ails your spirit, it's fun to take. There are no big pills to choke on, no foul-tasting syrups spilling from a spoon, just good old-fashioned fun! Play actually grows your brain, and it quiets down your limbic system. It helps you have more resources to heal old wounds.

What do you like to do for fun that uses your imagination? Maybe you like to paint or dance. Maybe you like to come up with new moves on your skateboard. You get the idea. Go do more of it—every day, if you can. You will be doing yourself and your brain an enormous healing favor.

Another way to help heal old wounds is to practice stillness or mediation. It isn't always easy to quiet the body or mind, but it's worth trying. Gurus and monks who meditate have better functioning brains and more loving, compassionate hearts than people who are busy and in a hurry all the time (like most of the rest of us). Practicing stillness not only grows the part of your brain that helps you make good decisions but helps you feel more love and peace.

Either learn a meditation practice (get a book, or google "meditation," and see which ones you want to try) or just *be* still. All you have to do is lay down for a few minutes. Start with five minutes and work your way up to thirty if you can. You don't have to move anything—not even a facial muscle. If your brain is still going ninety miles an hour, that's all right. Just keep your body still. Try it. It calms you down.

You can apply the movie mode you learned to deal with your Itty Bitty Shitty Committee when you are practicing mediation or stillness. Instead of just watching your negative thoughts, you can simply notice any of your thoughts and let go of any emotional attachment to them.

Just as being still can calm the mind and body, so can its opposite: movement or exercise. Exercise helps your brain create "feel-good chemicals" called endorphins. You need them to be happy and less stressed out. Ever notice how you get so involved in swimming a few laps or riding your bike, for example, that you forget about time passing and even about your worries? Exercise is like mediation in motion. It helps clear your mind.

Movement also helps your brain deal with your growing-up wounds. Dr. Peter Levine, a psychologist from Colorado (and the creator of Somatic Experiencing, a special form of therapy) explains that animals in the wild rarely suffer long-term effects from trauma even though they are traumatized by predators every day. They don't suffer long-term effects because they release the trauma by moving; that is, they shiver and shake after another animal has threatened them. Movement helps people release trauma when they let their body do what it feels like it needs to do. You may want to tremble, shake, jump up and down, or even cry after an event that makes you feel bad.

You may choose one or, even better, a combination of all three methods, but however you decide to help heal yourself, know that there is no instant cure. Be patient and keep at it. You'll notice a difference in time. Taking time to heal your wounds is a great way to learn how to be your own best friend and how to take care of yourself so you are able to be there for others.

You know the routine that flight attendants go through before every take-off? They show you what to do in case the plane loses cabin pressure, and those funny little masks fall down. The flight attendant then places the mask to his or her face and shows you how to put it on. And what does he or she tell you to do if you're flying with children or some-one who needs help with the funny little mask? Put your own mask on—in other words, take care of yourself first—before you start helping others. You can't help your child or someone who needs help in an emer-gency if you don't have what you need first (in this case, oxygen).

The same is true with life here on the ground. If you want to be a Dream Girl, if you truly want to be of help to others, you have to remember to take care of your own needs, too. You have to put the mask on, breathe deeply, and figure out who you are, what's true for you, and what you really want.

> **DR. JENN SAYS...**
>
> *I play to heal and grow my brain. You can too!*

Then and only then can you turn to a guy—or anyone else, for that matter—and say, "I'm there if you need me. I can help you if you want me to." Then and only then are you a *whole person*, with a whole lot to offer.

WHICH OF YOUR QUALITIES ARE YOU INVITING OTHERS TO SEE?

Every day, you hand out an "invitation" for others to believe certain things about you. You invite them to believe the things about yourself that you believe about yourself.

Of course, you have two invitations, one filled with negative beliefs and the other with positive beliefs. Some of the negative things you believe may be from your Itty Bitty Shitty Committee and others may be from your growing-up wounds. It doesn't matter how they got onto your invitation. What matters is that you work on healing them and work on handing out a positive invitation to others. There are so many positive things about you. Trust me. It's just that we often pay more attention to the negative things or invite them to stick around.

Let's look at your negative beliefs about yourself first.

In the following space write down all of the things you believe about yourself that are bad, inferior, etc. Write as many as you can think of. Maybe you think you are clumsy or stupid. Be as honest as you can.

Write down what *you* believe are your negative attributes—not what other people say about you or project onto you. Write from your heart in the space below.

 *My Negative List*

Now take a look at what you've written. What you see before your eyes is one of your very own invitations. These are the negative things that you put out for others to see, when in reality you have a much better invitation to give others. Ask yourself, is this really what you want others to believe about you? What are you willing to work on so that you invite others to believe the positive things about you?

Now it's time to write down what's really important: all the good things about you. Write at least twice as many things as you did for the negative list. Go ahead. It's perfectly all right to toot your own horn and remind yourself that you are great! No one is going to peek over your shoulder and tell you that you're stuck up or conceited because you believe good things about yourself. Actually, I dare you to write *triple* the number of negative things you wrote about yourself. Can you do it? I'll bet you can! Write them below:

 *My Positive List*

This is your positive invitation that you can hand out to others to believe the good about you. Now, every day when you wake up, decide which invitation you are going to "hand out." Are you going to invite others to see the negative things you believe about yourself rather than the positive ones? The choice, of course, is up to you, but I would hope you hand out the positive invitation. When you invite others to see your best qualities, you are also giving others permission to see the best in themselves so that they in turn will hand out positive invitations.

what guys want you to know:

Girls who invite guys to see their best get the most respect.

Secret No. 3

All of us have a dark side and a bright side. It's normal. Dream Girls know that guys will take them more seriously and have more respect for them when they invite others to see their bright side—their best side—not their worst.

Here's what guys have to say about the invitation you hand out:

What Guys Are Saying About What Girls Think About Themselves

I wish girls understood that if they think they are horrible, guys will too. We follow their lead.
    —Kyle, USA

Girls who want me to think of them as victims or helpless or stupid don't get my respect. Why would I want to be with a girl who doesn't believe in herself?
    —Shane, USA

*If you want me to believe you are good person, you have to
believe you are a good person; otherwise you want me to believe a lie.*
—Steve, England

VALUE YOUR VALUES

Your values are the things that matter most to you, excluding material things of course. If you're not sure what your values are, take a look
at the list below. Check off the ones that best describe what matters most
to you. Add others if necessary.

- ❏ Achievement
- ❏ Advancement and promotion
- ❏ Adventure
- ❏ Ambition
- ❏ Affection (love and caring)
- ❏ Arts
- ❏ Being around people who are open and honest
- ❏ Challenging problems
- ❏ Change and variety
- ❏ Close relationships
- ❏ Community
- ❏ Competence
- ❏ Competition
- ❏ Cooperation
- ❏ Country
- ❏ Creativity
- ❏ Decisiveness
- ❏ Democracy
- ❏ Ecological awareness
- ❏ Economic security
- ❏ Effectiveness
- ❏ Efficiency
- ❏ Ethical practice

- ❏ Leadership
- ❏ Location
- ❏ Loyalty
- ❏ Logic
- ❏ Meaningful work
- ❏ Merit
- ❏ Money
- ❏ Nature
- ❏ Order (tranquility, stability, conformity)
- ❏ Personal development
- ❏ Physical challenge
- ❏ Pleasure
- ❏ Power and authority
- ❏ Privacy
- ❏ Public service
- ❏ Purity
- ❏ Quality relationships
- ❏ Recognition (respect from others, status)
- ❏ Religion
- ❏ Reputation
- ❏ Responsibility and accountability

❏   Excellence

❏   Excitement

❏   Fairness

❏   Fame

❏   Fast living

❏   Financial gain

❏   Freedom

❏   Friendships

❏   Growth

❏   Having a family

❏   Helping other people

❏   Helping society

❏   Honesty

❏   Independence

❏   Influencing others

❏   Inner harmony

❏   Integrity

❏   Intellectual status

❏   Involvement

❏   Job tranquility

❏   Knowledge

❏   Security

❏   Self-respect

❏   Serenity

❏   Sophistication

❏   Spirituality

❏   Stability

❏   Supervising others

❏   Time freedom

❏   Truth

❏   Volunteer work

❏   Wealth

❏   Wisdom

❏   Work under pressure

❏   Work with others

❏   Working alone

❏   _____

❏   _____

❏   _____

❏   _____

❏   _____

❏   _____

Your values, just like the invitation you hand out, determine how guys see you. Your values help determine if you are a Dream Girl or a just-in-his-jeans girl.

If you value honesty, obviously you will be honest and attract love and respect. You will invite people to see you as trustworthy and loyal. But what if you value power or ambition? Or money? Most of us value money. Those can be incredibly good values to have as they will help you succeed in life. But they can also have a dark side to them. They can make you take advantage of friends to get ahead or keep you from valuing people as you climb the ladder to success, stepping on others' fingers, toes, or heads! Or your desire to make money can cause you to do things to earn it that you will later regret.

It is important that you understand what your values are and what they say about you. If your values enable you to live your life while respecting the lives of other people, chances are they're the kind of values that will put you on the fast track to becoming a Dream Girl.

Take a moment to think about the words you checked or the words you added as your values. *Are they respectful of you and others? What do your values allow you to do?*

If you value power, for example, what are your boundaries about power? How far are you willing to go to achieve power? For that matter, is it possible to live powerfully and still be respected? Sure, it is. Just look at Oprah Winfrey. Not only is she wildly successful, she uses her wealth and influence to promote education, create opportunities for young women, and accomplish other positive things that can help shape our future.

What, if anything, do your values keep you from doing? If you value friendship, you will most likely live a life that encourages friendships and stops you from damaging them. Hopefully, your values keep you from hurting yourself and others. Hopefully, they help you look again—make a U-turn—to see all the positive things about yourself and others. In a nutshell, let's hope your values help you *give and get respect.*

SELF-ESTEEM BY A MYSPACE GIRL

Girls can build up their sense of security by focusing on who they are, not on what they're going through or what the world tells them they are supposed to be. When a Dream Girl sets her boundaries before she gets into a situation where she might do or say something contradictory to her desires, goals, and values, she'll be a lot more willing to say no.

I wish girls realized that they are worth so much more than what today's world tells them they're worth. Stereotypes tear us down, and can cause us to give in to feelings of low self-worth, because it is easier to than to fight for who we are and what we deserve. However, not all girls know who they are or where they stand. If they've never had positive role models, they will find it difficult to recognize their own worth and inner beauty.

Here's what one of my MySpace friends, who also happens to be named Jennifer, has to say about this very subject:

> *Though I don't know what I want to do with my life, I know who I want to be when I'm older and how I want to get there. I know if I would focus more on how I treat others, then I wouldn't have to focus so much on how I am treated. If we treat people well, then what can they possibly say against us? If girls were just secure enough to treat one another right, to build each other up rather than tearing each other down, then confidence would not be so rare.*
> —Jennifer, USA

GUYS RESPECT GIRLS WHO

Guys have a lot to say about this, too. Here is a sampling from guys who answered my survey question, "I respect girls who _____"

> *Earn it by showing strong character.*
> —Eric, USA

> *Who aren't slutty and are friendly.*
> —Erin, Ireland

> *Know who they are and don't believe they are better than everyone else. They make their own life and live it like they want to.*
> —Tim, USA

> *Listen, don't judge, do not constantly gossip or talk smack, and are genuinely easy and fun to be around.*
> —Nicholas, USA

> *Speak their minds.*
> —Christian, USA

[Are] independent and don't feel they are less or more than anyone; they are real.
      —Sergio, Brazil

Are respectful, open-minded, committed and have a life.
      —Nicholas, USA

Respect their bodies and have values they stick by.
      —John, USA

Are laid-back, trusting and understand how a relationship should work [and who] want to learn and know there is never an end to learning.
      —Joe, USA

Know what they want to do, don't go by their looks, and go by their true feelings; don't dress like whores; and are themselves, open-minded, and trustworthy.
      —James, England

Listen to me, respect me, see me as a person and not someone who is just talking to them.
      —Josh, USA

Think of themselves as beautiful and one of a kind. Someone who knows who they are and doesn't have to imitate other people, [and who] carries themselves well and knows what they are about.
      —Kyle, USA

Are loyal and act decent in public.
      —Caleb, USA

Respect me, listen to me, and help me out.
      —Casey, USA

Don't care what other people think of them, are confident, and aren't afraid to get their hands dirty.
—Nathan, USA

Know what they want.
—Miles, USA

Don't have anything to prove and aren't high-maintenance and have a developed sense of humor.
—Harry, England

[Are] kindhearted and devoted to a relationship.
—Kundeel, Tonga

Aren't afraid to be themselves.
—Josh, USA

[Are] nice and polite to me.
—Mathew, USA

Carry themselves properly and are respectful.
—Kyle, USA

Work hard, look for a guy, and show love and kindness.
—Curtis, USA

Are intelligent and aren't afraid to show their feelings and are sexually comfortable with themselves and willing to admit faults in themselves and in me.
—Greg, USA

Know what they want and aren't afraid to try and get it, even if they know the chances are slim.
—Josh, USA

*Have some discretion with whom they date and have sex with
[and who] try to maintain some modesty in their lives and
look for guys who want to develop relationships and not a
quick screw.*
　—Jonathan, USA

SELF-RESPECT FEELS GOOD ... REALLY, IT DOES

Our bodies are mysteriously wise. They respond to our emotions.
When you feel sad, your body reacts by feeling sluggish or even sick.
When you feel good about yourself and you have a healthy attitude about
who you are and treat yourself with respect, you feel happier and more
alive than ever before. There's an energy to self-respect that makes us
feel so good, we want the rest of the world to know it.

what guys want you to know:

*Guys are attracted to the
energy that comes from a girl
with self-respect.*

Secret No. 4

What does self-respect feel like to you? Think of the last time you
were really proud of yourself. What sort of sensations did you feel inside
your body? Did they make you want to smile, dance, sing, jump up and
down, or even do a backflip or a cartwheel? Take a moment to think
about how self-respect feels to you; then write it down on the following
page. The beautiful thing is that self-respect feels different to everyone,
so there's no right or wrong answer.

Memo to Me:
Self-respect feels like...

Knowing what you feel like inside when you have self-respect is a great way to quickly know when—and why—you aren't in self-respect mode. You can then decide how and what you need to get back on track to feeling self-respectful.

Do you already know ways in which you aren't respectful to your-self? Knowing what you need to work on is half the battle. With that in mind, fill out the following Memo to Me:

Memo to Me:
I know I'm not respectful of myself when...

Don't worry if you discover that you don't always practice self-respect. Of course, that's the ultimate goal, but remember that you, and I, and every single one of us, is a work in progress. The road to self-respect is a journey, not a destination, just like life itself. It takes years and years to fully understand ourselves. Life might throw you a curveball now and then. Take your self-respect along with you, and be ready for what comes at you.

DR. JENN SAYS...

Developing self-respect is a lifelong process.

DISRESPECT IS A MISUNDERSTOOD EMOTION

It's easy to say that disrespect is the opposite of respect. But there's a lot more to it than that.

Disrespect is what happens when you do not hold yourself or others in high esteem, or when you do something violent to yourself or others. Violence as I'm defining it means anything that causes any kind of harm, be it physical, emotional, psychological, or spiritual. Sending a nasty text message and leaving a rude comment on a public forum page or someone's profile are not just disrespectful actions but forms of violence when you get down to it.

Disrespect usually, and often deliberately, creates fear and hate. Disrespect is also one of the sneakiest, most deceptive, and most misunderstood emotions on the planet.

You know what happens when your boyfriend makes you mad: you not only remember exactly how you felt but also the exact moment or the exact thing he said that set you off in the first place. And if you're like most couples, chances are the thing that ticked you off may have seemed like a little thing to him, but it felt like a big thing to you. For whatever reason, it made you feel slighted. You may have reacted in anger, but if you stop and look deeper at what your boyfriend said, you may eventually realize that what caused the anger, was you felt disrespected. That's part of what makes disrespect such a misunderstood emotion. It hides underneath your anger or even your fear.

The other problem with disrespect is that we can figure out when we feel we have been disrespected, but we don't always realize when we disrespect others. As a result, we may often end up hurting others feelings, or stirring up old wounds when that's the last thing we intended to do.

Here's a story from a junior high student that illustrates this very point:

> *I met this guy named Mike. He was in my biology class. I got up the nerve to talk to him after class one day. We had just sat through a long exam. I asked him how he thought he did, and he went off on me! He told me it was none of my business. He wouldn't talk to me. I had no idea what I did wrong. I was just trying to start up a conversation with him. One of my friends saw what happened, and they told me that he was really struggling with the class and that his parents were always on his case about his grades. He must have felt I was making fun of him asking about the exam. I had no idea that would feel disrespectful to him.*
>
> *I got up the nerve the next time we had class to talk to him about it. I told him I didn't mean anything by the question, and I certainly wasn't trying to be disrespectful. I was just trying to get to know him.*
>
> *It took a lot of guts for me to talk to him like that. I didn't know if he was going to go off again or what. But he was really nice about it. He looked a little embarrassed and told me he was sorry he had gotten so angry. He let me know how bad he was feeling about his grade in the class and how stupid he feels. He told me he thought everyone knew he was the "class idiot," so he thought my question was dissing him. We became pretty good friends after that. I even helped him study before the next exam.*
>
> *I am so glad I tried to talk to him again; otherwise I would have written him off as just a jerk.*
>
> —Alyse, USA

Your comments to people might just make them feel disrespected because of their battles or battle *wounds*. Mike's battle was his embarrassment over his performance in class. His anger was the signal that he felt disrespected, even though that wasn't Alyse's intention.

The best way to make sure you know if someone feels you have been disrespectful is to keep an eye and ear out for signals like anger, sarcasm, violence, or even silence. If you pick up on one of these reactions, chances are that disrespect is lurking around somewhere. Dream Girls know to look and listen for warning signs of disrespect in others. Instead of retaliating with anger or sarcasm or some other negative reaction, they know to ask questions and find out what is at the heart of the situation. It's not always an easy thing to do, but Dream Girls make the effort.

> **DR. JENN SAYS...**
>
> *Anger, sarcasm, avoidance, and violence are all warning signs that you or others feel disrespected.*

GUYS GET HURT TOO

We all need to be loved and respected. Sometimes it may seem like guys are tough and macho, and they don't need a lot of love and respect, but the truth is, for humans to grow and survive, we need to be loved, respected, and valued. We all need to feel that someone is there for us and that we have significance. It doesn't matter what your gender is. Guys may hide the fact that they have feelings about wanting to be loved, but they do.

> ## what guys want you to know:
>
> *Guys don't like being disrespected any more than you do. Dream Girls know that showing a guy simple respect goes a long way to helping him attain what he needs to grow and thrive.*
>
> Secret No. 5

When surveyed, most guys claimed that being disrespected by a girl caused them a great deal of pain and/or anger. Not many claimed that they didn't care or that they let the disrespect just roll off them. Here are some of their answers to the question "Being disrespected by a girl made me _____."

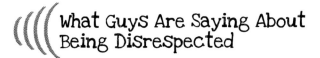

What Guys Are Saying About Being Disrespected

I became a bitter person when it comes to relationships and emotions. Being beaten down a lot is a real killer to my mental state. I am a very easygoing emotional person, and I tend to be able to deal with a lot, and after being beaten down so many times, it starts to wear on me and change my mentality towards girls, relationships, and life.
—Nicholas, USA

Feel hurt but mostly angry.
—Travis, USA

I lost all faith and trust in women.
—Shannon, USA

Being disrespected has caused me to wonder why I was treated that way. I know now that it was probably something that happened in her life that made her go on the offensive that way, but, at the time, all I could think of was what have I said or done to make her treat me this way. I reacted by just shutting up and letting her push me around, and that is not like any other relationship I had been in. I believe in a two-way street approach: both people have to treat each other with trust and respect, or it doesn't work. Disrespect leaves a lasting wound on you because it makes you feel like crap. It makes you wonder if the next relationship will be that way. It means

you watch over your shoulder with every new girl looking to
see if they have similar signs.
—Neil, Canada

It's a Dream Girl who has self-respect and shows respect to others. And it's the Dream Girls who get respect in return. They are taken seriously and are valued for who they are, not just for what they can do in the sheets and then be discarded. Guys hold on to Dream Girls. They know they are worth having around.

To sum up, here are the differences between Dream Girls and just-in-his-jeans girls when it comes to respect. How do *you* measure up?

DREAM GIRLS	JUST-IN-HIS-JEANS GIRLS
• Work to achieve self-respect	• Don't bother working to gain self-respect
• Know their past growing-up wounds can get in the way of self-respect	• Are clueless about their growing-up wounds
• Learn how to silence their Itty Bitty Shitty Committee	• Feed their Itty Bitty Shitty Committee so that it grows bigger
• Show respect to guys	• Disrespect guys
• Know that guys may seem tough on the outside but understand they can get deeply hurt and pay attention to not hurting them	• Don't pay attention to how they hurt guys
• Understand that, to get respect, you must give respect	• Feel that guys should respect them no matter how they treat the guys
• Know that respect is the key ingredient to an incredible future	• Do not understand that respect is the way to a better future

If you already have a lot of Dream Girl characteristics, that's wonderful. You will learn even more as you read the rest of this book. If you have more characteristics of a just-in-his-jeans girl, do not despair. This book is your guide to learning all the secrets guys want you to know so you can become a Dream Girl.

In the next chapter, you will learn about one of the most powerful skills you can use to place the Dream Girl crown on your head and shine your best. It is something that you were never taught in school, and I bet your parents never taught you, either. There's kind of an urban legend about it that keeps people from truly understanding it. Now, you can be one of the first girls to learn how to practice this skill that will attract guys love and respect and *keep them attracted*. Read on.

The Lost Art of Listening

"A girl who knows how to listen well does not need to worry because the relationship will go far."
—Robert, England

Robert's right. Listening is the key to any good relationship. Listening involves a lot more than just muting your mouth and turning up the volume on your ears. It also means knowing what to say that will encourage a truthful conversation when it's your turn to talk.

Even the most cutting-edge gadgets can only take you so far. Whether you're trying to conduct business, communicate with your friends, or set up a date with a guy, at some point you have to meet one on one—or, at least, speak to each other directly over the phone. Even in today's high-speed, instant-access world, it's still impossible to communicate clearly unless we listen to each other. We need to hear someone's tone of voice and see their body and facial expressions. When we talk face to face, special kinds of neurons, called mirror neurons, fire in our brains, and we are able to feel empathy for the person we are talking with. Empathy is what helps connect us as human beings. You can't get that connection reading a message or even hearing a voice mail.

Some people today don't understand that. I recently spoke to a young woman who wasn't sure where things were emotionally between her and her ex-boyfriend. She texted him, asking if he wanted to see a movie the next day.

He texted back, "Yes."

She Fandangoed tickets and texted him the movie time. He texted back, "Let's go." She was so excited they were going out.

Unfortunately, she received a text message from him the next day saying he was backing out: "Can't make it. Sorrrrrry!!!"

She asked me what I thought the message meant. Did the six r's in "sorry" mean he really wanted to see her but something unexpected came up? Perhaps the three exclamation points meant he really still cared for her, but he had to cancel?

I told her it was hard to know what he really meant. They needed to talk, not text, about it. And most importantly, when they did talk, she needed to listen. It's hard enough to get communication right when we talk face to face with someone, let alone try to interpret what someone might mean by words they type to us. Miscommunications like this can easily be avoided if we only knew how to talk and listen to each other. Yet, because many of us rely so much on our high-tech toys, we've completely forgotten how to do that. As a result, it's no stretch to say that the ability to listen effectively has become a lost art.

That's unfortunate, because as we're about to see, listening effectively is as important to becoming a Dream Girl as knowing how to respect yourself and others. It's another jewel in the Dream Girl crown.

I asked hundreds of guys ages fourteen to twenty-four to answer the question, "Who would you rather have a relationship with: a hottie or a girl who is a great listener?" Ninety-eight percent responded, I'd rather be with a great listener. That statistic is so impressive, it bears repeating. Ninety-eight percent chose being with a good listener—someone willing to show them respect by listening to what they had to say—over being with a hottie.

Now you may say, "If that's all there is to it, Dr. Jenn, then I got it made, 'cause I'm a really great listener. I've been listening all my life."

Really? I ask you to think carefully about your listening skills. Were you ever taught how to listen? Did you ever take a listening skills class? Most likely not. Of the four slices of the communication pie—reading, writing, listening, and language—the one we use more than the other three combined is listening. Yet listening is the one slice of the pie that isn't taught in school. It's not that your teachers forgot to teach you listening. It's just that our ability to listen has always been considered something that goes hand in hand with our ability to hear. In other words, the assumption was, if you can hear, you automatically know how to listen. It's kind of like an urban legend we've all come to accept, except that hearing and listening are not the same at all. Think of how many times you have told someone something important and they didn't get it. They heard the words, but they really weren't listening to you. They didn't take the time to understand what it was you needed or wanted. It's frustrating, isn't it? So if no one ever taught you how to listen, how do you know you're doing it right? How do you know if you're a good listener or a really bad one?

Now, you say you're a good listener. I am sure you know that listening is like any other skill or exercise: you need to practice it every day to remain effective. Otherwise, it's easy to develop bad habits.

"I'm sorry, Dr. Jenn, I musta spaced out. What were you saying?"

I'm saying it's time we take a closer look at the lost art of effective listening—what it means to really listen to one another—as well as the seven bad listening habits that can blow up your chances of becoming a Dream Girl.

what guys want you to know:

Girls who know how to listen well will have more meaningful relationships.

Secret No. 6

DETECTIVE LISTENING

Listening is more than just taking in sounds. It's taking those sounds and understanding where the person you're listening to is coming from, especially when those "sounds" are the thoughts, ideas, passions, beliefs, and deepest, darkest secrets that another human being shares with you.

Even if you don't completely agree with a person's thoughts, ideas, passions, beliefs, and deepest, darkest secrets, true listening means you respect their point of view.. After all, it's not your ability to hear the sounds that's important but, rather, your willingness to value another person's thoughts, ideas, passions, beliefs, and deepest, darkest secrets because you value that person and value his or her presence in your life, whether he or she is a friend, spouse, boyfriend, girlfriend, life partner, or, for that matter, a total stranger.

Remember how important respect is? Well, girls, listening is the ultimate show of respect. Listening is about opening your heart and connecting with another human being without trying to change, fix, make that person wrong, or belittle them. You do not have to agree with their viewpoint, but, rather, you understand that we are all different, and you are chill with that. As theologian and professor of pastoral counseling, David Augsburger once observed, "Being listened to is so close to being loved that most people don't know the difference."

DR. JENN SAYS...

You didn't learn how to listen in school, but you can learn now!

No wonder so many guys looking for love today place such a high value on listening.

So where do you go to learn how to listen if listening isn't taught in school? Not only is the answer simple, it requires little more than your imagination.

Pretend you're a detective: Nancy Drew, Veronica Mars, Brenda Johnson, or whoever you want to be. Now ask yourself: what's the most important thing a detective does to solve a case? You got it. She listens. When she interviews a suspect, she pays attention to everything—the things the suspect says and, just as important, the things he or she doesn't say—because she knows people's answers to her questions will provide the clues she needs to eventually crack the case. That is, she will uncover the truth.

Dream Girls listen like a good detective. They listen for the truths that can help them develop greater respect and understanding of the guys they like and want to get to know or fall in love with. They ask questions, are curious to know more, and make it safe for a guy to say what he really feels or really means.

Oprah Winfrey, recognized as one of the all-time great communicators, once said on a show that you can find on her twentieth anniversary DVD set, that everyone asks, "Do you see me? Do you hear me? Do you get me?" In other words, everyone's brain is hardwired in such a way that we want to know whether we "matter" or "count." And when it comes to close friendships or intimate relationships, we all need to know whether our friends or loved ones will be there for us or not. When you listen like a detective—or practice what I call "detective listening"—you let a guy know you are there for him.

HOW TO BECOME A DETECTIVE LISTENER

Detective listening can lead to successful relationships not just in romance but in all aspects of everyday life. It's a skill that begins with the intention of truly understanding—or "getting"—the person speaking to you.

Detective listening requires that you:
- Not make assumptions
- Stop talking so much
- Ask more clarifying questions
- Resist the urge to interrupt the speaker
- Resist showing anger or expressing criticism
- Do not hijack (steal) the other person's story
- Pay attention and don't just pretend to listen
- Don't give unwanted advice
- Don't get defensive

While not everyone can become a good detective, anyone can become a good detective listener once they master a few simple skills. And, as you can imagine, girls who practice these detective listening skills are well on their way to becoming Dream Girls.

what guys want you to know:

Guys have respect for girls who know how to be "detective listeners."

Secret No. 7

Detective listening means giving a guy your full attention. No wandering. You let him speak his mind, and you listen for content, not the delivery style. You don't crash the conversation or hijack the story he is telling you. Detective listeners listen for ways in which guys are different than they are and are at peace with the differences. Detective listeners do their own "emotional homework," which means they keep their issues in check so as not to instigate fights with a guy over words that could trigger feelings of anger. They also know to talk less and listen more, because, like a good detective, they know that listening often leads to the kind of truths that are really worth discovering. And they know that listening is respect in action.

For instance, let's say you're on a date with a guy named Dave. You've just ordered dinner, and, while you're waiting for your meal, Dave mentions that he really likes the band My Chemical Romance. As it happens, you are a huge MCR fan. You own all their CDs and have seen them live in concert; you post comments on the MCR fan blog, dream about Gerard Way, and basically eat, drink, and sleep everything MCR.

If you're a girl who practices detective listening, you will resist the urge to hijack the conversation into an opportunity to tell Dave everything you know about MCR—and believe me, we all know people who do that—and instead let him tell you how much he enjoys their music first. When you listen like a detective, not only will you discover that you both have MCR in common, but you'll probably discover other important things about Dave, like how he dreams of learning to play the guitar like Ray, or how he believes that better safety could have prevented Bob from burning his leg, or why the song "Cancer" makes him afraid his mom's breast cancer will come back.

The opportunity will arrive for you to talk about what MCR means to you. At a natural point in the conversation (like when he asks, "So what do you think of MCR?" or "Which bands do you listen to?") Dave will let you know that he is surrendering the spotlight, and now he wants to listen to you. Now you can talk about your mutual interests, as well as get to know more about Dave and his guitar-playing dreams, his ideas about safety for filming music videos, and his fear for his mom. What's more, you've formed a basis for a possible long-term connection. You'll have a chance to get to know each other on a deeper level, the level where real relationships start.

PLEASE JUST LISTEN TO ME

Detective listeners are slow to anger; they avoid criticizing guys, putting them on the defensive, or saying things that make them look bad. They do not impose their opinions on others or offer unasked-for advice. Instead, they ask questions, knowing that if a guy wants their opinion, he will invite them to express it through his answers to the questions they ask. And above all, they give a guy their complete and undivided attention. They turn off their cell phones and do not take calls or text messages from someone else while listening to a guy talk. No one likes to be ignored or "put on hold" like that.

A detective listener understands that the words a guy says are but a sliver of the things he needs or wants. So she does some gentle sleuthing of her own to determine the truth of what he wants her to know; and when she discovers that truth, she holds it in the highest regard. Even if she doesn't agree with everything a guy has said, a detective listener understands that the truth a guy has shared with her is the truth as the guy sees it. She does not attack him for it or defend her own viewpoint but, instead, recognizes it as his own.

It takes a lot of time and practice to become a good detective listener, but the payoff is well worth the effort. Detective listeners are highly valued by guys, as well as friends, family, bosses, colleagues, and, eventually perhaps, their children. Detective listeners have more success in life because the better they are at listening, the greater is their capacity for love and respect. After all, as we've seen before, listening and loving are close to being the same thing!

Take a look at this heartfelt plea found on the Internet from an anonymous teenager. You'll see just how well it illustrates the value of being a good listener.

When I ask you to listen, and you start giving advice, you have not done what I have asked.

When I ask you to listen, and you start telling me why I shouldn't feel the way I do, you are invalidating my feelings.

When I ask you to listen, and you start trying to solve my problems, I feel underestimated and disempowered.

When I ask you to listen, and you start telling me what I need to do, I feel offended, pressured and controlled.

When I ask you to listen, it does not mean I am helpless. I may be faltering, depressed, or discouraged, but I am not helpless.

When I ask you to listen, and you do things that I can and need to do for myself, you hurt my self-esteem.

But when you accept the way I feel, then I don't need to spend time and energy trying to defend myself or convince you, and I can focus on figuring out why I feel the way I feel and what to do about it. And when I do that, I don't need advice; just support, trust, and encouragement.

Please remember that what you think are my irrational feelings always makes sense if you take the time to listen and understand me.

What Guys Are Saying About Listening

I would say listening is the most important part of a relationship, and it's a reason why I cannot find many women that I like—because they talk but don't listen.
—Cori, USA

Listening is 50 percent of communication, an ingredient absolutely vital for a relationship. You can always say what's on your mind, but if you choose not to listen to your partner, their needs won't be met; and nobody wants to have an upset partner. We all know if a partner is upset long enough, you're going to lose them one day.
—James, USA

Listening is a lot like respect: you have to listen if you want to be heard, give to get. The better listeners you and your partner are, the better you can meet one another's needs and desires and work through all your relationship difficulties.
—Christopher, USA

I think it's very important to listen in your relationship, even if it's about petty things. The petty things are what make your relationship. And if you don't listen, what is the point in being in a relationship? There will be no trust.
—John, USA

Listening is one of the key points in a relationship, as well as honesty. But listening is the key to them all.
—Howard, USA

I think that it's important for people to be heard, because when you're not heard, it makes you mad at the person who isn't listening. It's worse when my friends don't listen, because they

are supposed to be the people who want to listen to what you have to say and care about what you have to say. But when they don't, it really hurts.
　　—Tom, USA

Communication is the main basis in a real relationship that is going to last. You have to be open and honest and be able to talk about anything, no matter what it is. If you can't communicate feelings or thoughts, they are just going to build up and it will be just like a time bomb, waiting to go off. If you can't communicate, then your partner will think you're hiding something. Same goes for listening—if your partner doesn't think you're listening, they will think your mind is elsewhere. Communication is the start and basis for any relationship and can be the ultimate end of one as well.
　　—Jimmy, USA

Guys had a few things to say about girls who are good at detective listening, so listen up.

((((What Guys Are Saying About Girls who Practice Detective Listening

My girlfriend has always listened to me [as if she were a detective]. I always felt like I was in heaven whenever she would listen as we spoke. It made me feel very important, as though I have a very important place in her heart.
　　—Edmund, USA

Certainly, I have had many girls listen to me like this. It's beautiful. The more you talk to a person like this, the more you learn about yourself. There is so much energy bouncing back and forward between both of you, the conversation seems to flow quickly. Before you know it, honest answers are flowing

out of your mouth. If you can't listen like this, there is no hope for you to have a genuine relationship with me.
—Bede, England

Marry me ... I wouldn't go out with anyone else but a great listener.
—Christopher, USA

Oh, yes! My girlfriend is exactly like this, she is a perfect listener. The greatest thing about this is, if you're unable to express your feelings by words, those listeners have the ability to see what you want to say and can react perfectly. It's like heaven!
—Max, Germany

THE LISTENING LANDMINES: WHAT THEY ARE AND HOW TO AVOID THEM

Okay, you now know the basics about becoming a detective listener. But like every skill, listening must be practiced every day in order to remain effective. Otherwise, it's really easy to develop bad habits. There are seven, what I like to call listening landmines, that even detective listeners are prone to. They are:

- Motormouthing
- Posing
- Hijacking
- Instigating
- Wandering
- Crashing
- Worrying

These bad habits, if not avoided, can explode at any time and destroy even the best of relationships. Girls who recognize these bad habits in themselves and take steps to defuse them, will be in a much better position to avoid the listening disasters that can blow up their chances of becoming a Dream Girl. So let's look at each of them closely.

HOW TO SHUT OFF YOUR MOTORMOUTH

Motormouthing is when you talk way too much and don't listen enough. This landmine is one of the easiest to trip, especially if you're with a guy who tends to be quiet and shy. After all, if you're more outgoing than he is, it's easy to think it's okay for you to do most of the talking.

The problem is, just because a guy is quiet doesn't mean he doesn't like to talk. It just means he doesn't like to talk as much as you do. If you do all the talking, you will never get to learn all the things about a guy that he ultimately wants to share.

Then there's the girl who motormouths even when her guy isn't shy and quiet. She goes on and on, and her guy can't get a word in edgewise. No one likes to be around someone who monopolizes the conversation. It's rude. That's why guys find girls who are motormouths to be really, really annoying.

Do you think you may be a motormouth? Pay attention the next time you're talking to someone. See who does most of the talking. If it's you, stop talking and learn how to pass the conversation over to the guy who has been listening to you. How do you do this? Easy! Think like a toddler.

> **DR. JENN SAYS...**
>
> *To avoid being a motormouth, teach yourself to become as curious as a small child.*

Think of how many questions toddlers ask because they don't know very much and have so much to learn. They aren't afraid that they might look stupid if they ask something. They just ask. And guess what? You can, too, once you teach yourself to become genuinely curious about the guy you are talking to.

Think about it. When you are genuinely curious about something, it means you are interested and really want to know about it. It's important to you; otherwise, why bother asking? In the case of your guy, you have a sincere desire to learn more about him—the things that are important to him. That sincerity will come across not just in your questions but in the complete and undivided attention you give him as you listen to his answers.

If you still find yourself motoring on, you can simply stop and say, "I'm sorry, I have been talking too much." Pass the conversation on to the guy by asking what he thinks about the topic you're discussing. Then be quiet and let him talk. Ask questions about what he has discussed. That lets him know you're not only listening but are interested in his opinion. Just remember that a conversation flows back and forth, so it's okay for you to do some talking. If you just ask questions, you will come across like a drill sergeant. Talking to a drill sergeant is just as annoying as listening to a motormouth. Remember, the powerful thing about asking questions and talking less is that everyone, guys included, likes to talk about him or herself. When you show interest in a guy and ask him to share his thoughts, he will feel more respected and take more of an interest in you, while you'll be earning new jewels for your Dream Girl crown.

what guys want you to know:

Your sincere desire to learn more about a guy says more about you than any words that come out of your mouth.

Secret No. 8

Guys had some interesting things to share about motormouths:

))) what Guys Are Saying About Motormouths

Once I met a girl who talked soooo much, I walked away from her and left her chatting to thin air.
—Shane, USA

When a girl talks too much, I feel like they are self-centered and it's a one-way street. It's like you are there for her, but she isn't there for you. When you need to talk to someone, you won't go talk to her!
—Woody, USA

A girl I knew monopolized the conversation so much that I never got anything off my chest. I always left our dates feeling drained.
    —Joshua, USA

I am going out with a motormouth right now. She won't shut up, and she interrupts, too. I need someone to talk to because my best friend's younger brother has cancer. I go to the hospital to see him, and even though it's not terminal, it's very depressing ... She acts interested and asks "What's wrong," but the minute I start talking, she goes on a rant about how annoying her hair is, and then she won't let me talk. Also she won't let me hang up. When I say I have to go, she changes the subject. It's irritating like nothing else, and kinda hurtful, because it makes me feel like she doesn't care about me.
    —Greg, USA

NOBODY LIKES A HIJACKER

Hijacking a conversation is another listening landmine you really want to avoid. The trouble starts when you change the topic or even share you own similar story, so that the conversation becomes all about you.

Nobody likes a hijacker. Why? Because when you hijack a conversation, the implication is that what you have to say is more important than what anyone else has to say.

DR. JENN SAYS...

It's not about you. It's about learning about him and showing him respect.

Not only is hijacking disrespectful, it ticks people off. Dream Girls know that, which is why they do their best to listen to what a guy has to say instead of barging in on the conversation and stealing the show.

If you have a tendency to hijack, and want to do something about it, remember what the MCR fan learned in the example from earlier in the chapter. When you wait your turn and totally focus on what a guy is saying, you put yourself in a position to learn more things about him.

And because you're giving him room to talk, you're also letting him know that he can trust you. The more a guy feels he can trust you, the more encouraged he'll be to share his thoughts, ideas, passions, beliefs, and deepest, darkest secrets—in other words, the things that really matter to him. Once you've established that level of trust, girls, you can begin to build the relationship.

what guys want you to know:

Nobody likes a hijacker

Secret No. 9

Guys want to know they can talk to you openly and honestly without fear of being hijacked. If you can't listen without stealing the story, guys won't bother sharing their stories, their respect, or their hearts with you. Here are some of their thoughts:

What Guys Are Saying About Hijackers

I was talking about this one thing. When I finished speaking, she blew me off and started talking about some bullshit. I told her upfront she was rude. I gave her the boot and said, "Peace out." She isn't a girl I even want to waste a day on.
—Mike, USA

No sooner had I said something, and she was on to something else, telling a story about something in her life completely unconnected with what I had just said. If I affirm your feelings in a conversation, you should have the decency to affirm mine.

*I still respected her, but her prospects to becoming my eternal
mate were slim to none.*
—Graham, USA

*I was with a girl for six years who was a hijacker, and it killed
me. After I told her she did it, she would still do it!*
—Josh, USA

IT'S BETTER TO SAY NO THAN TO POSE

Posing is pretending to be someone you aren't. Posing as a listener is
one of the landmines and that is really disrespectful. When you act as if
you really care about what a guy has to say, when nothing can be further
from the truth, that's so not cool. Think about it. How would you react
if you bared your soul in front of your boyfriend, only to find he wasn't
listening at all? It doesn't matter whether he only pretended to listen
because he was really tired, preoccupied with other thoughts, or just not
interested at all in what you were saying. You'd still feel the same. You'd
be upset, and you'd want to let him have it, right? Well, that's exactly
how guys feel when you only pretend to listen to them.

Dream Girls try their best to listen like a detective. But even the
sharpest, most compassionate detective listener can't be expected to
listen to everything, especially when she's not at her best. Sometimes
you need to unwind, refresh and recharge your batteries.

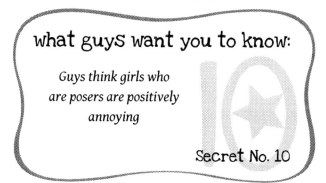

what guys want you to know:

*Guys think girls who
are posers are positively
annoying*

Secret No. 10

The problem is, sometimes it's hard to say no. Imagine it's late at
night, after a long day, and all you really want to do is to draw a hot bath

and soak in the tub for the rest of your life, when your cell phone rings, and it's your guy. He's really bummed about the long day he's had, and he wants to tell you about it. So even though you're practically brain dead, you let him talk and kinda sorta listen as you drift off in the tub, because you're afraid if you tell him you're tired, he'll think you're just like all those other girls who blew him off when it really mattered most.

Now it's possible you may be right. Some guys are quick to judge, just as some girls are. But most guys who were surveyed said they would rather a girl be honest and upfront and say she is too tired or too busy to listen than to fake it. So in the above example, it would be best to say, "I'm sorry, I want to hear everything about your day, but I just got home and I need to clear my head a little. Can I call you back in half an hour?"

Believe me, most guys will appreciate your honesty. They'd much rather wait thirty minutes or however long it takes for you to unwind and be at your best again. When you speak honestly like that with a guy, you're reminding him that you really do care about hearing him out. If you didn't care, you'd just let him blather on while you pretended to listen.

Pretending to listen while talking on the phone is not only easy to do, it's something we've all been guilty of, at one time or another. In this multitasking world we live in, it's easy to pretend we're giving the speaker our complete, undivided attention, when in fact we are doing homework, surfing YouTube, answering comments on MySpace, tweeting on Twitter... anything but fully listening.

DR. JENN SAYS...

Faking it doesn't cut it when it comes to listening.

It's much harder to pose in person, but girls still do it. Can you remember a time when someone sat right in front of you and looked like he or she was listening? The person nodded from time to time or maybe even held eye contact with you or sometimes smiled as if he or she was agreeing with what you were saying, but you knew deep down, he or she wasn't paying attention. Guys can tell when you aren't into what they are saying, no matter how hard you try to look as if you're giving them your full attention. Posing in person really shows a level of disrespect for people.

Guys won't take you seriously if you don't take them seriously enough to really listen to them. Dream Girls understand that, which is why they'd rather say no to listening to a guy once in a while than risk coming across like just another shallow, uncaring, inattentive, and, ultimately, unreliable just-in-his-jeans girl.

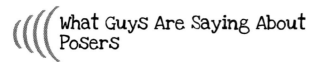

What Guys Are Saying About Posers

Posers make me feel like an inch tall.
    —Scottie, USA

I have had girls pose, pretend to listen to me so many times. I can tell when they are doing it, and I feel it is disrespectful, so I pretty much go tell them to screw themselves because they aren't listening.
    —Cody, USA

Posing hurts the most because it shows that girls don't care, period.
    —Rolando, USA

WORRIERS WORRY ABOUT EVERYTHING EXCEPT HOW WELL THEY REALLY LISTEN

Worriers are listeners who mean well, but they're actually too self absorbed to listen effectively—especially when they're with a guy. That's because worriers trip out over everything: how they look, how they feel, what a guy thinks of them, whether they're being too cute or too funny or too serious or too intense or too morbid or too offensive or too … whatever. They obsess over not knowing what to say or about saying the right thing or the wrong thing, or how clever they will sound or how stupid they will sound and whether they will please the guy they're talking to in the first place. What they're doing is worrying too much. What they aren't doing is listening!

In a way, worriers have a special kind of IBSC; only these itty bitty thoughts are ones that prevent worriers from listening to other people. Instead of focusing all their attention on the guy they're with (like a good detective listener would), worriers focus on themselves. They spend so much time worrying about themselves or what they're going to say next, they miss out on what's going on right now, right in front of their ears and eyes.

Now it's normal to be a bit concerned about how a guy perceives you when you and he are talking—especially if it's a "first time," you know, like when you first meet or go on a first date or even talk on the phone for the first time. It's normal to want to please a guy you want to get to know or are crushing on and to want him to like you back. Believe me, even I worry about how people perceive me when I begin a seminar or a Dr. Jenn's PJ Party, or even when I first start working with a client. We all want to make a positive first impression.

what guys want you to know:

Guys wish girls would stop worrying about themselves and pay more attention to them.

Secret No. 11

The trick, of course, is to not let our collection of itty bitty worries consume us to the point where it becomes obvious that, while we may be there for a guy in a physical sense—as in sitting right next to him or right across from him—we're certainly not there in a mental sense. So how do you do that? How do you manage to put your own thoughts and worries aside so that you're back on track and ready for conversation?

First, work at silencing your Itty Bitty Shitty Committee. That will make you a much better listener in the end.

"Yeah, but Dr. Jenn, how can I listen to a guy and go into movie mode?"

You can't. Being in movie mode means you are focused on your own thoughts, simply watching them without any judgment. You can't possibly pay attention with your ears and heart to a guy's thoughts when you are busy paying attention to your own. But you can practice what I call "beginner's ear." Beginner's ear is when you pay attention to the present moment in a way that is open and curious. It holds a sense of wonder and the possibility of discovering something new while you focus on ever finer detail. Remember what it was like when you were a young child, and everything was new and fascinating? You were just beginning to understand the world and people around you. When you are curious about things and using your ears as if for the first time, it's hard to stay focused on your own thoughts. You're curious about who the person you're talking to is and about what he or she might want you to know. You listen deeply and pay close attention.

One way to think about beginner's ear is to remember what it was like when you were a little girl. Can you remember hearing the sounds of the night and not knowing what they were? You listened carefully and paid attention to the small details. Perhaps you first heard a branch brush the window. That got your attention, and your ears perked up with curiosity. What was that noise? Since it was new, your ears just beginning to understand and make sense of things, you listened more intently. And then you were able to hear the chirp of crickets or maybe the small creaks of the house as it settled down for the night. It was your curiosity that made you pay attention to the finer details. That is the heart of beginner's ear. When you are curious, and you listen as if you are listening for the first time, the details become important. It's really hard to worry about yourself when you are intent on discovering the small details about a guy.

The more you apply your beginner's ear to each conversation with your guy, the more you'll hear things you might not have heard before. The sharper your beginner's ear—the more attuned you are to the things he wants you to understand about him—the sooner you'll find yourself out of your head and into a place where you can be there for him.

A Dream Girl knows how to use her beginner's ear to focus on what her guy wants her to know about him. Guys value girls who give them their attention. They don't value girls who are constant worriers, as you'll see from their comments on the next page:

((((What Guys Are Saying About Worriers

Being listened to by a worrier made me feel like I didn't have to take the conversation seriously.
   —John, USA

I have been around a worrier before. It made me feel like I was her older brother, and she wanted to learn from me. All I wanted to do was to get to know her. She always told me what she thought I wanted to hear. I didn't start the relationship to make a clone of myself. I started the relationship so I could get to know the person under her shell. I never found that person, and the relationship never worked out.
   —Bede, England

I have a story about a worrier. I met this girl at my freshman orientation night where all freshmen get to see what high school is all about. We eventually started talking online. As we got to know each other, she started asking me questions like, "Do I look okay?" A few weeks later, I realized she was a little egocentric. I broke off our relationship, and she became my stalker! She kept on following me around at school asking me questions at random points in our conversation, like "Do you like my pants? My hair? My shirt? Oh, wait! What about my shoes?" It got to the point where I couldn't take it anymore. I talked to her and learned she wanted to please me all the time. We finally worked things out, and she has learned that she doesn't have to do that anymore.
   —Tim, USA

*Worriers are annoying. It pisses me off that they try to listen
like that. I just want to have fun with the girl and be carefree. I
am supposed to feel like myself around her and she is supposed
to feel the same.*
        —Scottie, USA

INSTIGATORS ARE ALWAYS LOOKING FOR A FIGHT

Some people, for whatever reason, consider every conversation an
invitation for a fight. You know who I'm talking about: the kind of people
who never seem to be happy unless they're agitated or in an argument.
People like that are known as instigators. They are on the defensive in
every conversation.

Think how hard it is to be in a conversation with someone who is
always itching for a fight or always on the defensive, as if everything
he or she hears is an attack. When you fight or even defend, you can't
possibly understand what the other person wants you to know about or
what he or she thinks. You can't hear who he or she really is.

For a long time, that was the exact problem that plagued my friend
Katie.

Katie had been ignored by her mother for most of her life. Her mother paid
a lot of attention to Katie's brother and
sister, but, for some reason, she had a
hard time creating a solid, loving attachment with Katie. Her mother often put
her down, criticized her, and did other
things to Katie that made her feel badly.

> **DR. JENN SAYS...**
>
> *People can learn to stop
> being instigators and learn
> to heal old wounds*

This growing-up wound affected the way Katie listened to everyone,
including the guys she wanted to get to know better. She was always
listening for ways in which people reminded her of her mother, always
on the ready for a fight.

One day, the guy Katie had an enormous crush on sat down next to
her at lunch. She was thrilled to have his attention. Unfortunately for
this guy, he had barely said more than a few sentences when Katie went
off on him. He had no idea what he had said that upset Katie, but he sure

didn't want to find out. He immediately got up, left the lunch table, and swore that he would never talk to her again.

Fortunately for Katie, there's an upside to her story. Katie was so upset over losing the chance to get to know this guy better that she began to work on her issues and to change her listening style. She realized that everyone was not her enemy, out to hurt her like she had experienced with her mother. Although she blew her chance with her crush, she would have more chances with new guys in the future. She was determined to heal her wounds so that people would respect her again. She was willing to work at becoming a Dream Girl.

Go back to the growing-up wounds quiz from the previous chapter. Are you still hurting from old wounds? If so, you may also have words, phrases, or topics that trigger those issues, consciously or unconsciously, which means you may be susceptible to instigating fights whenever you hear those words, phrases, or topics, whether you know it or not.

That being the case, how do you defuse this listening landmine? It's a challenge, to say the least; but that doesn't mean it's impossible.

One thing you can do is simply become aware of what happens whenever you hear those triggers. One way to become aware of the feelings is to get to know how they feel in your body. What does anger, fear, shame, or any other emotion that gets triggered for you and makes you want to instigate a fight feel like in your body? Write those sensations below and on the next page:

Memo to Me:
I want to fight when I feel...

If you're with a guy, and he unwittingly says something that stirs up any of the sensations you wrote down, stop and take a deep breath—literally. Remind yourself that what you are feeling is tied to old wounds and that the guy who is talking to you is not the enemy. I know this means that you will have to take your attention off of him for a little bit so you can get a handle on your emotions, but that's better than going off on him. If you can tell him what's going on for you and that you are upset but you know it isn't his fault—that its old stuff for you—that's fabulous. But it's hard even for adults to be that clear with others, so don't sweat it if you aren't able to go there. Just being aware that the past can make you want to go ballistic in the present will help. The more you are able to recognize what makes you want to instigate, and the more able you are to breathe through it, the less charge it will have in the future.

Guys really get annoyed with instigators. Fighting wears guys out, and when they are that worn out, they can't see that you are trying to polish your Dream Girl crown. Chances are, you look more like a just-in-his-jeans girl, and that's not what you want.

What Guys Are Saying About Instigators

I get very, very annoyed with instigators unless I say something directly offensive. There is no reason to argue. If you are that angry about life, you should find someone responsible to take it out on or seek therapy. I am not your adversary or intellectual punching bag. This is potentially a relationship, not a competition.

—Tariq, Brazil

This, to me, is the worst type of listener. I had a girlfriend I fought with constantly. Ironically, it was my longest relationship, but I have never felt so degraded in my whole life. She took away who I was from me and changed me to the point [that] every one of my friends noticed. I actually hate this girl just thinking about her. Hate and love are the strongest two words in my life. That is why, when I say hate her, it means something to me. In a year and a half, I was never right once. She sometimes argued just to hear herself talk. And when things didn't go her way, she would turn on the water works. And me being the pleaser that I am, I would be right there for her. I find this type of listener to be manipulative. No guy wants to fight about every little thing.

—Neil, Canada

I had a girlfriend who had serious problems in the past. She didn't actually blame me but gave me the feeling that I was responsible for everything bad that happened. She really searched for arguments and possibilities to hurt me. I had no other choice but to end the relationship.

—Max, Germany

WANDERERS NEED TO EXPLORE THE WORDS
THAT CAN GET THEMSELVES BACK ON TRACK

Wanderers are listeners with chronic short attention spans: they just can't pay attention to anyone or anything for very long, no matter how hard they try. This, of course, can be hard to deal with if you're the guy the wanderer is supposed to be listening to.

Even though you may not be wandering on purpose, any guy who's really interested in you and who wants to make a connection with you can't help but wonder how much you really care about him when you keep zoning out. After all, nobody wants to be with someone who's not all there for them.

Wandering is not only a sign of disrespect; it can also send the wrong message. You can be the kindest, gentlest, hardest-working, and most compassionate would-be Dream Girl the world has ever seen, but none of that will matter if you can't overcome your inability to pay attention when people talk to you. Guys will dismiss you as a lightweight, airhead, bimbo, beezy, ditz, flake, you name it: the kind of girl he'll never take seriously enough to think of you as girlfriend material.

That nearly happened to a girl named Michelle.

Michelle was a wanderer who wanted to get to know a guy named Louis. But whenever she tried listening to him, her mind went in a zillion directions. Luckily for Michelle, Louis was not only a good sport about this, he was a great guy with a great big heart who really cared about her. He realized Michelle didn't mean to be rude and always managed to steer her back on track. He would tease her, and say things like "Earth to Michelle" or ask her if she'd forgotten her ADD meds. Not only did that make Michelle laugh, it also got her to refocus.

Of course, not everyone was as kind as Louis. In fact, most of the other guys Michelle had dated were so turned off by her wandering, they completely blew her off. They didn't want to have her around as a friend, let alone a possible girlfriend.

That's why wanderers often have a hard time building healthy, respectful relationships. They certainly don't become Dream Girls unless they decide to change the way they listen and show respect.

I'm happy to say that Michelle got the message. She was so grateful to Louis for shedding light on her wandering, she begin to work hard at changing her listening style. Today, she's not only a better listener but a better person, with many new friends who recognize her many good qualities and who respect and love her.

Wanderers can stop their wandering the same way that posers learn to stop posing: by considering for a moment how the person who is talking to them feels. Ask yourself how you would like it if a guy kept tuning in and out whenever you spoke to him. Unless you come from another planet, you'd probably say, "That would suck."

If you find yourself wandering, the best thing to do is to admit it. Honesty is always the best policy when it comes to relationship issues, and communications problems are no different. Tell the guy you're talking to that you are having trouble staying focused. You don't have to explain why. Ask him to repeat what

> **DR. JENN SAYS...**
>
> *Wanderers can learn how to curb their wandering by becoming word explorers.*

he just said—the part that you happened to tune out on—and refocus with a renewed effort. You can also rephrase what he just told you (or at least, the part that you heard) to either let him know you were trying to listen, or make sure you understood what he has said. In other words, even if you didn't catch his exact words, you can always check for the meaning behind the words, because the words he uses are merely an attempt to explain what he needs.

Yup. That's right. When he talks to you, he is letting you know what he needs. When we speak, we usually are communicating a need of some kind. Sometimes they're big needs, and sometimes they're little ones, but they're all needs just the same. By checking in to make sure you know what a guy means, you'll be better able to understand what he needs.

It's not difficult at all to teach yourself how to curb your wandering and enhance your ability to focus. All you need to do is become a word explorer. Instead of exploring strange, new worlds and charting paths unknown, you're looking beyond the words a guy says in order to discover the meaning of what he really wants you to know and what he needs.

For example, let's say a guy asks you what you think about the new supercharger he installed in his car. In this instance, you couldn't care less about what's under the hood of his car or, for that matter, anyone else's. All you care about cars is whether yours will start when you turn the key in the ignition and how much your next trip to the gas station will cost. So you figure that maybe nobody would blame you if you zoned out this time around.

But the thing is, it's not the engine he just installed that's important, it's important that he told you about it in the first place. Knowing that, a girl who did some word exploring might recognize that the guy was interested in sharing something important to him when he talked about his car.

what guys want you to know:

Guys want girls to explore the meaning of the things they say.

Secret No. 12

Maybe what he wants to share is a relatively little thing, like "Now that I have this sweet new engine, I can go zero to sixty in no time." But maybe it's something much bigger, like a feeling of accomplishment: "I installed this engine all by myself. That's something I never thought I could do, and that makes me feel good." His need is for you to join in with him in his excitement about doing something he didn't think he could do. What matters is that it he wanted to share it with you.

Remember, guys today value the importance of good communication. But at the same time, they're ... well, guys. They don't always get things right the first time words come out of their mouths, so it can take a while for them to say what they really mean. Sometimes it takes an intuitive girl—a girl who practices word exploring, uses her beginner's ear and listens like a detective—to pay attention, to dig deep into the words a guy uses, and help him draw out what he needs you to know.

Dream Girls know that part of the fun about learning how to listen to a guy are the many treasures she'll find as she discovers some of the truths behind his words. So stop your wandering and pay attention.

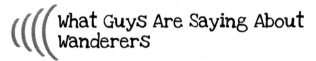

What Guys Are Saying About Wanderers

Girls who listen with a wandering style make me feel unimportant, that I am not worth their time. Why should I bother talking if she can't be bothered listening. It feels like she is kinda shallow.
—Sam, New Zealand

I had a friend who was a wanderer. I asked her if she realized she didn't pay attention to what I was saying. She couldn't follow and had no clue. That ended the whole friendship. I was very angry and disappointed that she wasn't in a frame of mind to keep our conversations more normal.
—Tony, USA

Unless I just want to get into your pants, I will get frustrated with your wandering and just move on.
—Jake, USA

CRASHERS ARE EVEN WORSE THAN HIJACKERS

Crashers are girls who interrupt a guy's conversation. Crashing is similar to hijacking, only crashers don't grab the steering wheel, change the course of the conversation, and run with it; they simply cut people off by injecting a quick thought in a way that kills the conversation altogether. They don't steal the conversation and never give it back; they chop into it because something someone has said creates an intense emotion in them. The feeling can be fear, anger, excitement, joy, or some other emotion that revs them. Crashers can't bear holding in their feelings until it's their turn to talk, so they jump right into the conversation.

Courtney was a habitual crasher. She would hear a guy talk about things she loved and couldn't contain her eagerness to join in the conversation, so she crashed it. Russell, a guy she liked, was telling her about his latest snowboarding run down Ajax Mountain in Aspen. He was so stoked about the run, he was talking with his hands and smiling from ear to ear.

But Courtney remembered her fantastic run down a California mountain last year and cut him off entirely. She kept interrupting him, saying "I know just when you mean. When I went down a run at Heavenly, I had the same feeling."

Every time Russell told her of an incredible turn he'd made, Courtney interrupted him with a quick comment that she, too, had had the same experience. It wasn't too long until Russell stopped telling her his story. He got tired of being interrupted. It would have been better for Courtney to hear his full, entire story and give him a high five for his incredible maneuvers on the slopes. Then, with her heart full of her own memories, she could have asked if Russell wanted to listen to her story. Then they would have had something in common to share, and he would have felt heard and respected. Courtney would have looked more and more like a Dream Girl, not some rude crasher who didn't show a guy respect.

Some girls crash not because they can't contain their emotions, but because they are simply impatient. They don't understand—or aren't willing to understand—that some people talk slower than others, have a harder time expressing themselves than others, or may even have speech impediments, such as stuttering, that affect their ability to articulate their thoughts as well as others.

If you're a crasher, none of that matters. You just want to get to the point and share your point of view, the sooner the better. That's why girls who crash often finish sentences for guys whether the guys want them to or not. If you have ever found yourself at a loss for words or stammering, you know how embarrassing it can be for someone to finish your thoughts or to say the word you are fumbling for. Crashing is so commonplace in most cultures that it takes a good deal of self-awareness to stop it. But it's worth the effort, especially once you realize just how disrespectful it is and how much guys hate it.

Crashing, like hijacking, sends the message that "What I have to say is more important than what you have to say." If we were to explore those words even further, we'd also find that crashing tells a guy you think you're more important than he is. Even if you do want to become a Dream Girl, if you tend to crash conversations, you'll create the impression that you're just another self-centered, just-in-his-jeans girl who couldn't care less about winning a guy's heart—when nothing could be further from the truth.

Here's another example of why a lot of Dream Girls-in-training crash and what you can do about it.

Let's say a guy is ticked off over something you said. You ask him what's wrong. In the course of explaining why he's so upset, it becomes apparent that, whatever you said, he took it in a way completely opposite of what you actually meant. You so can't believe how wrong he took it, you can't think straight or sit straight. All these emotions are bubbling inside you, to the point where it makes you uncomfortable. All you want to do is blurt out, "I can't believe you feel that way." So instead of patiently waiting for your turn to talk, you jump in and defend yourself.

On the one hand, you feel a whole lot better. You've had your say; you've made your point. On the other hand, not only is the guy still ticked off, you've made the situation a whole lot worse because it can now escalate into a full-blown argument.

If you can hold your tongue, wait to hear everything he has to say, remember to be curious and ask questions, and empathize with him, you will walk down the red carpet of Dream Girldom with light bulbs flashing and people asking for your autograph.

Okay. That's a bit over the top. But really, girls, if you can avoid crashing when you want to defend yourself and instead listen to what your guy has to say, you will learn how to grow a very healthy relationship.

I snuck in a word to test your detective listening skills in that example. Did you find it? Yes, it's empathize. Not only should you ask questions, you should get in your guy's shoes and take a stroll around, feel what it's like to be him for moment. That's what empathizing is: you try to feel what another person feels. If a guy is angry with you, even if it is for something you didn't say or do, or if he took what you said the wrong way, he is still angry. It doesn't matter much at that moment whether his truth and your truth match up. Let him tell you his version, and let him know you feel him.

Girls, I know how hard this can be. But that's what Dream Girls do. We acknowledge that what the speaker is saying is their truth and that how they feel about it is the way they feel about it.

Once you let people know you are there for them, they can begin to calm down and listen to what you have to say when the time is right for you to say it. So instead of crashing with "I can't believe you feel that way!"—which only stops true communication from happening—let your guy talk until he is done. Ask questions about how he came to the conclusion he did about what you supposedly said or did.

But use caution. Remember, you are asking questions to help you understand his point of view, not interrogating a prisoner. And watch your body language. Make sure it isn't saying, "I am sooo angry with you!" Find out what his truth is. Then, when it's your turn to talk, you can let him know you are sorry he took

> **DR. JENN SAYS...**
>
> *Mirror what you want to have come back to you.*

things the wrong way and begin the process of explaining your truth and your point of view about things.

Want to know why it's important to ask questions in a nice voice and to avoid facial expressions or body language that say, "I am angry" or "You're an idiot"? Okay. Here are some more brain facts that Dream Girls need to know.

Remember the mirror neurons that fire when you speak face to face that you learned about earlier in Chapter Two? When you hear or see someone else expressing an emotion, your mirror neurons fire up, and you mirror back, or feel, similar feelings. So if a guy is bitching you out for something, you most likely want to jump into the ring and fight back because your mirror neurons are mirroring his anger. If you are aware this is taking place, you can take a deep breath and respond to him calmly and curiously. You can empathize with him and let him know you get that he is upset.

When you are calm, kind, and respectful in your response to him, guess what? His mirror neurons fire up, and they mirror your calm, kind, respectful mood. Bingo! You have avoided a fight and have helped him calm down. Guys adore girls who don't throw gasoline on an already raging angry fire but, rather, help guys put out the flames and calm down.

If you have done a supersleuth's job at finding out what his truth is about the situation and have acknowledged that he is furious about it and responded calmly, he will be more willing to listen to your version of the truth and feel respected, even though you may disagree.

Another tip from psychological research: most guys are not as verbally gifted as girls. Some guys flounder or stutter when they talk about deep emotions. Or they mumble. Or they say things in ways we don't process as they do. So give your guy the time and space he needs to process his thoughts and find the way to express them. If you don't, you'll make him feel like you're mothering him (which is something he'll resent). Not only that, the words you put in a guy's mouth may not be the words he's looking for to express the thought, idea, passion, belief, or deepest, darkest secret he needs to tell you. In that case, all you've done is derail him from sharing the truth he wants you to know.

Learning how to curb your crashing will go a long way to helping you become a Dream Girl. Guys will take you far more seriously and have much more respect for you when you allow them to share their thoughts and feelings without fear of crashing.

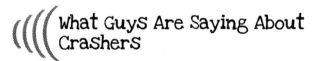

What Guys Are Saying About Crashers

I have been around crashers. Every time I spoke, she was just waiting for something she could relate to so she could jump in and turn the conversation back to herself. It got to the point where I just confronted her. I said, "Um, I am not sure if you

are trying to be rude, but it would be nice if you could let me finish what I am saying before you jump back to the subject of you."
　—Paul, New Zealand

I've had girls crash my conversations many times; it really upsets me. Grrrrrr! I hate it more than anything else in conversations.
　—Mike, USA

People who tend to interrupt have no remorse, so I stop talking to them. If they feel like what they have to say is more important and they have to say it, they should at least have the respect to wait until I'm done talking. But that never seems to happen.
　—Kyle, USA

If you want to be considered as a Dream Girl, practice your detective listening skills and avoid the seven listening landmines whenever you can. Not only will that show your guy how much you respect him, it will most likely prompt him to return that respect to you!

THE LISTENING LANDMINES QUIZ

Now that we've discussed all seven of the listening landmines, take the following quiz. Which ones do you tend to detonate? Circle all of the numbers below and on the next page that describe you:

1. If something I have to say is important, I speak up and cut others off.
2. I get bored easily, and so I just pretend I am listening.
3. I don't like to give up the conversation. I do most of the talking.
4. I find myself saying things like, "I know what you mean," and then talk about my situation that is like the one the person is talking about.

5. I get really anxious when I talk to a guy. I just want to make him happy so he will like me.

6. I want people to think I am listening to them, so I look them in the eye, but I am really not listening most of the time.

7. Sometimes people tell me stories that remind me of my own experiences, and I stop the conversation to tell them about my story.

8. I hear things that I disagree with or make me angry, and I have to show the other person that he or she are wrong.

9. I think I must have ADHD, because I tune in and out of conversations.

10. I listen for topics or words that I know make me angry so I can talk and prove my point.

11. I hate waiting for someone to get the point, so sometimes I finish their thoughts for them.

12. If I get excited, I will cut someone off in mid-sentence.

13. I can't focus on what people are saying. I just wander off.

14. If the conversation isn't about what I want to talk about, I will change topics really fast.

15. Guys just sit there! They won't talk, so I do.

16. Some people need to be straightened out. I tell them when they aren't right.

17. I know my friends want me to listen to them, so I just nod and say "Uh-huh" a lot. I don't really pay attention.

18. Who's got time to focus on one conversation? I listen, text other people, and can't be bothered to stay with just one conversation.

19. I just agree so people don't get mad at me.

20. I worry about how much a guy likes me instead of listening to what he has to say.

21. I talk more than the guy I am talking to does.

If you answered numbers 2, 6, and 17, you are a Poser.
If you answered numbers 5, 19, and 20, you are a Worrier.
If you answered numbers 1, 11, and 12, you are a Crasher.
If you answered numbers 8, 10, and 16, you an Instigator.

If you answered numbers 9, 13, and 18, you are a Wanderer.

If you answered numbers 3, 15, and 21, you are a Motormouth.

If you answered numbers 4, 7, and 14, you are a Hijacker.

Each landmine has three examples in the quiz. You may have only circled one instead of all three. That means you have a tendency toward that landmine, and you might not be setting off that landmine on a regular basis. Or you might be.

If you're like most people, your answers may show you to have a combination of several listening landmines. For example, you may be a hijacker who also tends to worry or an instigator who also tends to crash. Many girls find that they have circled at least one answer from each landmine. That doesn't matter. What's important is that you're taking a long, hard, objective look at areas of listening in which you know you can be better, so that you can do something about it. Believe me, not only will guys appreciate your desire to improve your listening skills, so will everyone else.

Check out how you compare to a Dream Girl or to a just-in-his-jeans girl when it comes to listening. What things do you want to work on changing or improving?

DREAM GIRLS	JUST-IN-HIS-JEANS GIRLS
• Talk less, listen more	• Motormouth until a guy's eyes glaze over
• Put their tongues to the roof of their mouths until it's their turn to speak	• Make it hard for a guy to get a word in edgewise
• Are confident enough they can focus on what a guy is talking about	• Worry about everything and can't take in what a guy is telling them

• Know it's respectful to wait their turn before they share their ideas, points of view, stories, etc.	• Can't contain their emotions or need to correct or finish a guy's thoughts and crash the conversation
• Work at healing old wounds so they are not carrying around angry baggage	• Hear words that trigger old wounds and instigate fights
• Practice detective listening	• Set off a lot of listening landmines
• Give guys their undivided attention when listening	• Pretend they are listening
• Focus on what a guy is saying	• Wander off and on, not paying much attention to what the guy is saying
• Listen for needs and meaning underneath the words a guy says	• Can't be bothered to get to the heart of the matter
• Understand that listening is respect in action	• Think that multitasking while listening is okay
• Know that listening is another foundation to building a healthy relationship	• Think they are already great listeners. Not interested in learning how to be detective listeners to show respect
• Let a guy tell all of his story	• Hijack conversations

Detective listening is key to building a respectful relationship. But there are times when acting like a supersleuth, or more to the point, a super snoop, can actually harm your reputation and relationships. It all comes down to trust. Find out how you measure up as trustworthy in today's world of communications technology, and more, in the next chapter.

Building Your Trust Account

"Trust is like a vase—once it's broken, even though you can fix it, it will never be the same."
—Donald, USA

Trust ranks right up there with respect when it comes to building good, strong, long-lasting relationships. Without trust as part of the foundation, there's just no way to expect a relationship—*any* relationship—to be built to last.

"Oh, come on, Dr. Jenn! I *know* trust is a big issue in relationships. What in the world could you possibly write about trust that I don't already know?"

Great question. Well, sure, everyone knows that trust is a fragile commodity, especially with intimate relationships. It can take weeks, months, even years for two people to establish a level of trust and understanding with each other; yet those same two people can shatter that trust completely in a mere instant. And like our friend Donald says in the quote above, once trust is broken, it's almost impossible to put it back together exactly as it was before.

Sure, all the basic things about trust and relationships that my generation dealt with, like not cheating on your partner or not telling lies, still hold true today. But your generation has new issues to deal with that can impact your relationships.

Your generation has a more complex relationship with trust than any group before you. The convenience of modern technology adds complexity to your relationships and can invite suspicion to what may be a truly innocent situation or, in fact, create trust-breaking situations. Part of the problem with relationships today is that, along with all of this new technology, we have a whole new set of guidelines about trust—so many guidelines, in fact, that it's hard to know which behaviors are considered trustworthy and which ones are not. Consider these questions:

- Do guys care if their girlfriends send flirty text messages or e-mails or engage in "cybersex" with other guys? Is that really cheating?
- Do guys care if you create a profile on a dating site like True.com to lurk through profiles and "wink" at hot available guys, even if you never intend to meet them face-to-face?
- If you message an untruth, does that count as much as telling a lie face-to-face?
- Is it okay to use a guy's password to check his messages on his cell phone, e-mail, MySpace or Facebook account without his consent if you think he is cheating on you?
- Is it okay to demand that a guy give you his password as a "sign of trust" when you are going out?
- Is it okay to use his password just to check up on him even if you don't think he is cheating?
- Is it okay to change his password and lock him out of his messages until he comes clean and tells you what he has been up to if you have suspicions about his behavior?
- Is it okay to use his password to delete messages you think he shouldn't be listening to or reading, such as messages from other girls?
- Does leaving mean comments on someone's MySpace profile or Facebook wall lower your trustworthiness?
- What happens when you write an in-your-face, "F.U." message,

you know, the kind you would never have the guts to say face to face to someone?

- How do guys feel if you ignore a message from them?
- Do guys trust girls who continually check up on them with calls or texts?

CAN HE TRUST YOU TO BE IN HIS SAFE TRIBE?

Let's start with the basic, old-fashioned trust issues. Believe it or not, the one thing guys want to know most about a girl is not "Will she have sex with me?" but rather "Can I trust her?"

Guys may not always say it in so many words, but that's what they want to know. Even if you are only going to be friends, guys want a commitment from you—a commitment that tells them you will be nice to them, kind, loyal, respectful, trustworthy, and loving. In other words, guys want to know that you'll treat them right. They want to know if they can count on you to be there for them.

> ## what guys want you to know:
>
> *Guys want you to know that they need to be sure they can trust you—today, and every day.*
>
> Secret No. 13

Guys constantly have their trust radar turned on to help them determine who belongs in their safe tribe. A safe tribe is that select group of friends that we know we can trust whenever we let down our guard—no questions asked. Everyone has a safe tribe, guys and girls alike, even if it's a tribe of one or two people. Guys want to give you their trust, whether they see you as a possible romantic partner or simply as a good friend. They listen and watch for ways in which you are trustworthy, as well as for ways you might be ruining their trust in you.

So what does a girl do to show a guy that she is worthy of being in his safe tribe? Learn how to be trustworthy in every situation. That's not always easy, since it's a crazy world out there. So let's sort it all out together. But first, let's hear what the guys have to say:

((((What Guys Are Saying About Trust

Trust is built by solidarity and love. "If you feel me" may be the worst grammatical phrase out there, but it best describes what it takes to build a trusting relationship between a man and a woman. It takes a give-and-take relationship, with the number one most scarce human speech pattern being honesty and another rare one called actual conversation involving listening and then talking. What breaks [a relationship] is lying about anything, cheating, and vindictive badgering to gain control in a relationship.
—Neil, USA

Trust is earned over time. It seems for me that the more I trust myself in the relationship, the more she can trust me ... and it comes full circle, and I trust her. But it can be broken obviously by cheating.
–Jared, USA

WE ALL WANT FAIR PLAY

Cheating is not only one of the most obvious ways to lose a guy's trust, it is one of the most time-honored ways of destroying a relationship—guaranteed. We all know what it's like to be lied to or treated badly by other people—even people we thought were our friends. We all know what it feels like to have our feelings hurt, our hopes crushed, our hearts broken, our trust betrayed. And even if we've been fortunate enough never to have been cheated on by our boyfriend, girlfriend, spouse, or lover, we all know people who have gone through the hurt of that painful, trust-breaking experience.

what guys want you to know:

Guys want girls to play fair.
No Cheating!

Secret No. 14

Back in the early '80s, a stylized negotiation was first studied by experimental economists Güth, Schmittberger, and Schwarze. It was called the Ultimatum Game, an experiment in economics that, as it happens, also has some interesting psychological ramifications. The purpose of the Ultimatum Game was for two people to decide how to divide a sum of money between each other. Neither player knew each other. All they were told was that they could keep the money *if and only if* they could decide how to split it on the very first go-round of negotiations. In other words, they only had one shot at dividing the money. They didn't get a second chance.

Here's how it would look: Player 1 must make an offer to Player 2 as to how to split the money. Let's say the sum is ten dollars. Player 1 might offer Player 2 only one dollar, hoping that Player 2 realizes that one dollar is better than nothing. If Player 2 accepts, Player 1 pockets nine dollars, and Player 2 gets only one dollar. Every one is a winner, right? They both have money they didn't have before.

But something curious happened in the negotiations. In many cases, Player 2 turned down amounts that he or she felt were too small—or in other words, unfair. When Player 2 said no to the offer, neither player got a penny. Player 2 felt that *nothing* was *better than being treated unfairly*. Not only that, by saying no, he or she punished Player 1 for offering an unfair amount (in this case, Player 1 lost out on his or her nine bucks).

You can see just how much the issue of fairness plays in this game. As a matter of fact, studies have been written about how the Ultimatum Game shows the extent to which people are willing to accept instances of unfairness, inequity, and injustice in certain situations. (If you are interested, google "the Ultimatum Game" and read more.)

Now here's the interesting thing. Studies have also shown that, in many cases, and in many cultures, people who play the Ultimatum Game usually offer a "fair" split; in other words, Player 1 offers Player 2 half the money, and assuming Player 2 accepts, they split it right down the middle. Obviously, people value fairness.

Whether it's a game of economics or the game of love, the rules remain the same: we all want to be treated fairly, guys and girls alike. And while there may not be monetary value in the game of love, that doesn't mean the stakes aren't high. After all, if you don't play fair, if you betray your guy's trust by cheating

DR. JENN SAYS...

Playing fair is the object in the game of life and love.

on him with someone else, you risk losing out on the high-interest yield of a loving, long-term relationship. People want their partners to play fair, that is, to remain faithful. Cheaters never win other people's respect. Guys hurt just as much as girls do when they find out they have been cheated on. If you find that hard to believe, read what happened to my friend Joe.

I loved a girl name Kerry. I met her when I was eighteen. I thought I had met my soul mate. Kerry understood everything about me. She listened with her whole heart when I talked to her. She made me smile even when I was having a bad day. She was always asking me how she could be supportive. I trusted her 100 percent. I even told my parents I was going to marry her. I just couldn't imagine life with anyone else.

Last spring, Kerry texted me to pick her up to take her home. She was over at our friend's house, hanging out with everyone. I didn't think anything about it, as we were all good friends. I got to my friend's house and a bunch of my buddies were hanging around the front yard. I walked to the front door, but one of them got in my way and started making stupid small talk. I was startled. I told him I needed to go inside and get Kerry. He just stood in front of me and kept on about some bullshit I didn't see the point in talking about. I started to get pissed off. One of my other friends walked over and started talking to me too, adding to the nonsense the other friend was telling me. I tried to brush them off and get around them, but they wouldn't let me get to the front door.

I got suspicious. "What's going on?" I asked them.

None of my buddies would answer me. I knew something was wrong, [especially since] all of my friends had this awful look on their faces.

I walked into the house and found Kerry and one of my friends putting their clothes on. Kerry gave me a look I will never forget. She just stared right through me like what she had done was nothing at all. My now ex-friend started apologizing like crazy. I told Kerry he could drive her home.

A while later Kerry called me and asked if we were still together. I hung up on her. I haven't dated since. I am too afraid to risk being that hurt again.

My buddies outside of the house told me they didn't know what to do, but they didn't want me to walk in on Kerry doing the deed. They knew I would have blown up.

I heard from some friends later that Kerry lost a lot of our mutual friends that day. No one trusted her anymore. And my ex-friend who tapped her, he wasn't too liked by the other guys, either. I think they were always afraid he would step in and go after one of their girls.

— Joe, USA

Joe's story isn't that unusual. Many guys have shared with me their stories about being cheated on, and quite a few said they don't want to date anyone anymore or that it took a long time to regain their trust in girls so they could try to date again. Their hearts have been broken, their trust shattered.

Dream Girls know that if you want to be considered trustworthy, you have to *be* trustworthy. Cheaters never win, and winners never cheat.

THE CHANGING FACE OF CHEATING

Girls cheat on guys for many reasons. Some are working out old growing-up pains at the expense of their boyfriends, while others have this compulsive need to feel wanted by other guys. Some girls cheat on guys just for kicks, while others justify their actions on the basis of revenge. You know, tit for tat. If he cheated on me, then it's okay for me to cheat on him.

I understand all of those reasons. But that doesn't make any of them right.

No matter what your reason for cheating is, it's still a no-win situation. At some point, the truth will come out ... *it always does*. And when it does, someone will get hurt, whether it's you, the guy you cheated on, the guy you cheated with, or all of you together. That puts a dent on your reputation that's even worse than being called a just-in-his-jeans girl. You're a *cheater*.

Guys view girls who cheat on guys as a risk to be involved with. If a guy knows you've cheated before in a relationship, why shouldn't he think that you will cheat on him? That's pretty straightforward. It certainly made sense when I was your age. The problem is, as we've discussed before, the world is much different today. Electronic communication and networking sites have completely changed the way we relate to other people. As a result, our ideas about cheating today have also drastically changed. Let's look at the first two questions you answered a few pages back.

Do guys care if their girlfriends send flirty text messages or e-mails or engage in cybersex with other guys? Is that really cheating?

Do guys think it's cheating if you create a profile on a dating site to lurk through profiles "winking" at hot available guys, even if you never intend to meet them face-to-face?

Now, not everyone will agree on the same answer, as everyone has a different opinion on what *real* cheating is. Some guys feel that only having some sort of physical, sexual encounter is real cheating; others feel that any flirting or giving your affection away to someone else in any form, real or virtual, is cheating. But all guys agreed that a virtual flirtatious relationship outside of the one you have with him hurts. You may think you're just playing, girls. But for many guys, just knowing that their girl is "carrying on" online with another guy—even if there is absolutely nothing going on physically, even if you've never actually met the person—is a serious form of disrespect. In other words, your relationship with the guy you're texting may be entirely virtual ... but the hurt it causes your guy when he finds out about it is nothing short of real.

what guys want you to know:

Many guys consider "cyber flirting" to be a form of cheating.

Secret No. 15

So what do you if you're a Dream Girl who loves to text almost as much as she loves her guy? Is it possible to enjoy your communications devices without screwing up your relationship and your reputation?

Sure, it is ... so long as the lines of communications between you and your guy always remain open. Set the guidelines as to what cheating means to both of you, and *stick to them.*

DR. JENN SAYS...

If you consider it cheating, he probably does too. If you don't know, ask him!

That means you have to have a serious talk in the beginning of your relationship about the rules you both agree to when it comes to the Internet or cell phones. It may well be that he's okay with you chatting online with other guys in certain circumstances, such as people you know from an online forum that you both belong to. However, if you are creeping around dating sites or profiles on Myspace or Facebook checking out other guys, don't be surprised if he considers those to be grounds for cheating. I assume *you* would, too.

Another guideline you can follow is to apply Dream Girl logic to the situation. If you think he might view your actions as disrespectful to you, him, or other people, then it's best to not take those actions. Whether it is "real" cheating or not, guys feel hurt when you make a connection with other guys that you have to hide from them. That is a big red flag.

This is so important that I'm going to highlight this for you: If you have to hide it, if you're ashamed to do it in any way ... *don't do it!*

After all, Dream Girls are all about respect. And respect doesn't ever have to be hidden or kept secret. Respect gets you loved, and that's what you really want, right?

What Guys Are Saying About Cheating

I found out my g/f was texting her ex, telling him she still liked him. I found out because one of my friends was with him when she texted him, and he told me. I felt terrible. She was texting both of us, telling us how much she loved us. I was, well, devastated. I mean, how can a girl play two different guys at the same time? She said she never hooked up with him after they broke up, but I didn't care. Her text messages were enough cheating for me! I dumped her ass.
—Robin, USA

Carole—I will call her Carole—was always putting up pictures of her and other guys on her [MySpace] profile. She always had cute little captions under them that seemed really flirtatious to me. When I asked her about them, she always blew me off. It got to the point I hated looking at her page, but felt like I had to just to see what she was doing. I mean, she posted them for everyone to see. What was I supposed to do? She claims the guys are just friends, and I know some of them are, from

her middle school years. But, c'mon, did she have to write cute little things under them, like she wanted to be with them and not me? It felt like she was cheating on me, even though technically she may not have been.
  —Anonymous, USA

I don't understand why girls have to cheat. I mean, if we don't make you happy, just break up with us. Don't hurt us more by cheating on us.
  —Brandon, USA

Once a girl I was in a long-term relationship with cheated on me with a friend of mine, and he told me. I ended up trying to forgive her, and she went and did it again. I have never felt so injured. Sometimes I worry that the experience ruined me for good as a partner. I was so much different before it happened.
  —Erik, Egypt

LIAR, LIAR, PANTS ON FIRE

Lying goes hand in hand with cheating. Of course, most cheaters lie to cover their tracks. But there are plenty of other things we lie about that have nothing to do with cheating. Some lies are bigger than others, and some cause more damage than others. Lying can not only instill feelings of mistrust, it can kill a serious relationship. Everyone knows honesty is the best policy; why not just speak the truth? We lie because we're afraid that we might end up being rejected or that we might hurt a guy's feelings, like the girl we met in the previous chapter who faked listening to her boyfriend because she didn't want to tell him she was too tired to talk. Or we may lie simply because we just don't want to admit we're wrong.

What about messaging an untruth? Is that different than telling a lie face-to-face? A lie is a lie, no matter if you type it or speak it.

It's usually best to message the truth. The only time to avoid messaging your truth is when you want to break up with someone, you are angry, or in other situations where your negative emotions have control of you. The truth still rules, but let it rule in a face-to-face conversation. It's okay to unleash yourself from technology once in awhile. Some topics simply don't translate to type very well, and besides, it's disrespectful to dump someone by texting.

It's also hard to sort out lies you have messaged someone. Remember what Sir Walter Scott wrote in his 1808 poem "Marmion"—*Oh what a tangled web we weave.* It's hard to keep track of lies. The truth is much easier to remember because it actually happened.

DR. JENN SAYS...

Telling a lie is self-serving: it takes care of your needs but not the needs of others.

Then again, there are times when telling a lie can actually do some good.

Imagine your best friend has a pimple on her face that she cannot do anything about. Do you recoil in terror when you look at her or suggest she put a paper bag over her head before she goes out into public? Or do you say, "No biggie, no one will notice?"

Most people would reassure their friend that her zit is no big deal and no one will pay any attention to it, no matter how gross it looks. This is what is commonly known as a little, white lie.

Dream Girls know the difference between little, white lies and the kind of lies that can upend your relationship: the ones that have to do with cheating, backstabbing, and withholding the truth for fear of hurting a guy's feelings. Those are the lies that can permanently derail Dream Girls on their path to finding love and respect.

WHAT'S TRUE FOR YOU?

It's not always easy to tell the truth, but by no means is it impossible. If you're a Dream Girl in the making who has trouble speaking honestly about relationship issues, one way you can improve your ability in that area is to understand your own truth.

Years ago, two brilliant women, Sherry Ruth Anderson and Patricia Hopkins, wrote a book called *The Feminine Face of God.* In it, they wrote about discovering that people who had built incredible lives had done so by asking two questions: (1) "What's true for me?" and (2) "What do I really want?"

Knowing what is true for you can often help you tell your truth to others. To illustrate this point, let me share a story that one of my MySpace friends shared with me. For reasons of privacy, we'll call her Brenda.

Brenda wrote that she had a hard time telling guys how she felt. She often lied to them to make them happy, only to let them down in the end. She wanted to change her pattern of behavior. Once she sat down and began thinking about what was true for her, she had a long list of qualities about herself that she understood better. She was able to tell guys that she was afraid of being hurt by them, and she stood up for herself instead of just telling guys what she thought they wanted to hear. Before long, she stopped lying to them and to herself. As a result, her relationships got better—and her reputation did, too.

You can understand your own truth too, just like Brenda did. As you read each question that follows, take some time to think about it; then write down your answer on the next few pages. Remember that this is for you and you alone. Be honest with yourself. You have nothing to lose:

 *What do I lie about most?*

 *What lie have I told recently that I could make amends about?*

Now I want you to answer those two powerful, life-changing questions: What's true for me? And what do I really want?

If you want to go deeper, ask yourself: What am I willing to do to get what I want and still live within my truth and values?

Don't expect all of the answers to arrive at once. Answering these questions is challenging and takes time. And over time, your answers may even change. As you grow, your truths and wants can change dramatically.

Write your answers under the questions on the following pages. If you want to add more thoughts, write them on another piece of paper and staple them into this book. Actually it would be best to keep a journal and write the questions in it and answer them on a regular basis. You can have fun discovering the answers. You can write long entries or just one or two words. You can thumb through old pictures, magazines, or books and cut out words, phrases, or pictures that depict your wants and truths and paste them on the page. The key is to have fun with it.

What's true for me?

 *What do I really want?*

*What am I willing to do to get what I want
and still live within my truth and values?*

Did you answer the questions? I hope you did. Guys want you to know who you really are, because then and only then will you know who you are in a relationship with them.

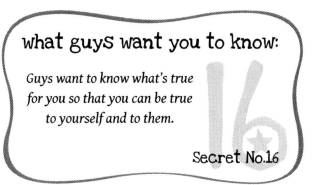

what guys want you to know:

Guys want to know what's true for you so that you can be true to yourself and to them.

Secret No.16

If you find yourself writing a lot negative things about yourself, go back and re-read parts of Chapter One and see if you can find some ways to boost your self-respect.

LIAR, LIAR, BRAIN'S ON FIRE

Years ago, there was a famous public service announcement about the dangers of drug abuse. Perhaps you've seen it posted on YouTube. The spot begins with a close-up of an egg, while the narrator says, "This is your brain." Then we see the egg cracked open and dropped into a hot skillet. As the egg sizzles, the narrator says, "This is your brain on drugs." As TV spots go, this one really hit the nail on the head when it comes to illustrating how much damage excessive drugs and alcohol use can have on the human brain.

Just as drugs and booze can alter your brain, so does excessive lying. At the time, it might seem like a good short-term solution to avoid rejection or pain, but lying raises your stress hormone levels, buries you in shame, and prevents you from exploring other behaviors that might otherwise benefit you.

For example, Carrie used her boyfriend's password to sneak into his cell phone to read his text messages. She was afraid he was getting tired of her and maybe was texting other girls. When he asked her if she had used his password, she lied and said no. Not only did she deny it, she acted as if his question was an accusation about her character and made such a big deal out of it that he felt wrong for having asked. (Liars often turn the tables and make the person they have lied to feel guilty for trying to uncover the truth.)

Carrie felt guilty that she had gone behind her boyfriend's back and even guiltier that she'd lied to him. She was ashamed of her behavior, but she didn't know what to do about it. She became hypervigilant around her boyfriend, afraid he would discover the truth about her lie. As a result, Carrie's limbic system—the part of the brain that triggers defense mechanisms once we feel threatened—became activated whenever she was with her boyfriend. When your brain is limbically activated, your body may feel shaky, or you might feel anger, fear, or any other negative emotion. Everyone has his or her own patterns of feelings. Carrie had a hard time connecting to the part of her brain that allowed her to make rational, logical life- and love-affirming decisions because her limbic system was activated.

Carrie would have been better off had she turned toward her initial feelings of concern that her boyfriend was getting tired of her and asked him about it. Had she turned toward him and her own truth, rather than turning away and going behind his back, she may have grown as a person and grown the relationship. Instead, she lied and shut down connections to her higher brain power.

In effect, Carrie damaged her brain—not physically, of course, but in the sense that her actions messed her up emotionally for a long, long time.

what guys want you to know:

Guys want you to know that even though it's stressful, it's always better to tell the truth.

Secret No. 17

Our brains function better when we are not limbically activated. Science now understands more about how our brains work. We know that being in a limbic dominant state doesn't allow you to have the proper neural connections to the part of your brain you need to in order to maneuver through life in the best way.

If you find that it's too stressful to tell the truth, one solution is to create a "safe tribe" of detective listeners that can help you learn to tell the truth and build a better trust account with guys and a better relationship with yourself.

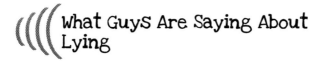

DR. JENN SAYS...

Turn towards the truth.

Learning to *turn toward* things that upset you, scare you, disturb you, or worry you is another way to learn to tell the truth, as well as to embrace other people on a compassionate, respectful level. When you want to tell a lie, turn toward the feelings that the lie is trying to cover up. Be compassionate about what you feel or what you have done and look carefully at what is causing you to feel or behave the way you do.

(((What Guys Are Saying About Lying

A girl who would consistently lie isn't worth dating. If you respected me, you wouldn't lie to me.
—Tony, USA

Girls, you don't need to lie to us. Okay, if [you] did something that you shouldn't have done, of course, we're going to get mad—we're human. Girls do the same thing when we lie about something.
—Will, USA

THE PASSWORD IS TRUST

Lying and cheating aren't the only issues of trust that concern guys today. Another form of mistreatment they commonly complain about is when their girlfriends do the very same thing that got Carrie into trouble: using their passwords to find out who they're messaging on MySpace, Facebook, or any of the other social networks that many of us frequent.

Five of the questions posed in this chapter dealt with password issues and trust. Let's take a quick look at them again.

Is it okay to use a guy's password to check his messages on his cell phone, e-mail, or MySpace account without his consent if you think he is cheating on you?

Is it okay to demand that he give you his password as a "sign of trust" when you are going out?

Is it okay to use his password just to check up on him even if you don't think he is cheating?

Is it okay to change his password and lock him out of his messages until he comes clean and tells you what he has been up to if you have suspicions about his behavior?

Is it okay to use his password to delete messages you think he shouldn't be listening to, such as messages from other girls?

How did you answer those questions? I hope you answered no to all of them.

"But, Dr. Jenn, how will I know he is cheating if I don't sneak into his messages to find out? I need to look at his accounts."

No, you don't *need* to sneak into his accounts; you *want* to sneak into his accounts. There is a difference.

As to how you'll find out if he's cheating, that's a good question. Maybe you won't ever find out, but as I said before, the truth *almost always* surfaces at some time. But by respecting his privacy, you will earn a great deal of respect for yourself and from other people.

I know it's hard to not know every little detail about what our guys are doing when they aren't with us, but that's where trust comes in.

If you can't trust your guy and you have to sneak around to find out what he is doing, you don't have a very solid relationship, do you? If you can't talk—and I do mean *talk*, not IM, e-mail, text, or voice mail—about your relationship and what each of you are doing, chances are your relationship won't last very long, because you don't have a foundation of trust.

Sometimes girls go beyond just sneaking around and checking up on their guys. They'll take it even further by deleting messages they don't like or don't want him to see, or even changing their guys' password or profile *without his consent*. This goes without saying, girls, but it's just not cool to do that. After all, it's not your MySpace profile: it's *his*. Going into his profile without his knowledge is not just a violation of privacy, it's a breach of trust, a *huge* sign of disrespect, and a possible indication that your relationship with each other may not be all it's cracked up to be. Think of it like you're using someone's bank card without his or her knowledge. You're not only breaking your guy's trust, you're also invading his space.

If you're concerned about who your guy is talking to online or on his cell, you need to talk to him face-to-face about it, honestly. Use no technological means of communication. And when he talks to you, you need to practice your best detective listening so that you understand where he's coming from.

what guys want you to know:

Jacking a password is a major show of disrespect.

Secret No. 18

However, be aware that it's possible some of the things he's going to tell you are not things you want to hear. For example, what if he tells you he *has* been texting other girls? Instead of freaking out about it and tearing him a new one (which, of course, is what you'd *like* to do), try to be calm. After all, instead of trying to lie to you, he's just told you the truth. So cut him a little slack. Soften your voice and ask him about his need to talk to other girls. Become curious about it. Ask what's going on. It takes an enormously loving, respectful girl to stand by a guy and say, "I may be hurt, but I want to help you figure out what's true for you. How can I help?"

This is not to say that you should become a doormat or a victim. After all, doormats don't do much to help anyone. They just take the dirt from the bottom of people's shoes and sit with it. Nor am I suggesting that you stick around if a guy is harming you in a way that is damaging to your body or is so toxic that it's damaging your heart and soul. I *am* saying that you should stick around and hear him out and see what his truth is, and then you can decide what to do.

Remember, a Dream Girl is a girl who wants to help. By letting her guy know she will be there for him, she gives him the chance to work out any issues he has that may be in the way of his own growth and the growth of the relationship.

As for demanding his password as a "sign of trust" so that he knows you can check up on him, that's really a sign that you don't trust or respect him at all. Now, if at some point he gives you his password on his own volition, that's another story. But demanding it as a sign of trust, devotion, or love is just as controlling as a guy telling you that if you really loved him, you'd have sex with him. No one likes being told we have to prove our love or trustworthiness. And if he does happen to hand you his password, that doesn't mean you have to use it.

Here's what some guys have to say about girls using their passwords behind their backs:

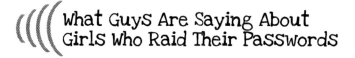

What Guys Are Saying About Girls Who Raid Their Passwords

> *My ex used my passwords to check my e-mail accounts, and the lack of trust that it showed hurt our relationship greatly.*
> —Tony, USA

Okay ... girls need to realize that when they act all controlling and try to use our passwords to read messages, giving other girls who look at their b/f dirty looks or anything else like that ... it just drives the guy away. That's what happened with my x-g/f. Girls need to realize that no matter how good they look, if they act this way, all attraction will be lost.
—Jaime, USA

I've had my heart broken, and I've been cheated on, lied to, and have had my g/f spying on me and checking up on me, and none of those relationships worked out. They could have, but they just didn't because of lying, deceit, and other problems. Those things do not work.
—Jon, USA

"I'LL GET BACK TO YOU AS SOON AS I CAN" (A QUICK REFRESHER ON IM ETIQUETTE)

We talked before about the flip side of modern communications technology: how even though these gadgets all come with instructions on how to use them, they should also include a warning over the many problems in *miscommunication* these devices often cause.

Take instant messaging, for example. These days, depending on what kind of device you have or which software program you use, you can IM someone through your laptop, desktop, cell phone, land line, PDA, or for that matter, even your television. And that's all good. As a matter of fact, more and more businesses use IMs to communicate with clients, staff, and employees, whether they're in the office or at a remote location. It's a really efficient way to send short messages to each other, whether at work or at play.

The problem with IMs is this funny expectation that when we send an instant message, we're supposed to receive an instant answer. And if we don't get an instant answer, something must be wrong.

Think about the last time you sent an instant message to your guy, but didn't get a reply right away. If you're like most people (guys and girls alike), it probably never crossed your mind that (1) he may have been away from his computer at the moment or (2) if it's a text message or a voice mail, he may have actually had his cell phone turned off at the time you sent the message. Instead, you got ticked off at him and took it as a slight.

Dream Girls trust their guys enough to know that, if they don't always get an instant answer to their instant message, there's usually a pretty good reason. And they know not to badger their guys about where they were, or who they were with or why, why, *why* they didn't answer right away.

It's okay if you don't always answer your phone or IMs pronto. It's another thing to ignore the message *completely.* It's entirely fine to wait to reply to an IM or text message because you are at the movies or in some other area where you can't receive a signal or are someplace where using a cell phone simply isn't appropriate.

Yes, my friends, there *are* times and places when using a cell phone is rude. For instance, if you came to my wedding, I'd be really upset if I knew you decided to take a call at the very moment I said "I do" to the man I love and respect. Or maybe you're out with your friends. Believe it or not, it's rude to hang with your buddies and text other people at the same time. I know your generation is great at multitasking, but think how you feel when you are sharing something deep and personal with a friend and she reads and answers a text while supposedly listening to you. This is a perfect time when she should ignore the text and wait to answer.

That raises one of the questions at the beginning of this chapter:

How do guys feel if you ignore a message from them?

Here's the answer:

When a text message goes unanswered for too long, the sender can often feel ignored, rejected, or excluded—in a word, ostracized. Research on ostracism has shown that being ignored not only decreases healthy feelings about ourselves but can have a negative effect on us psychologically. This is especially true when the sender and recipient happen to be romantically involved.

When you ignore a text message from your guy, you're telling him he doesn't matter to you. He may ruminate over it, wondering what he did wrong to make you ignore him. He may wonder if you're with another guy or if you've stopped caring about him or he may simply wonder what you're up to that is keeping you from answering him. Those are all normal reactions, but none of that helps him feel good about himself and the world around him. Unless the message he sent you is rude and crude (in which case, by all means ignore it), you owe it to him to reply. You don't have to break your neck to answer him right away, but it is good manners to get back to him as soon as it is convenient for you, even if you just touch base and tell him that you can't get into a conversation at the moment but that you will get in touch again in the near future to talk.

what guys want you to know:

Guys don't want you to ignore their messages or them.

Secret No. 19

Girls who simply ignore text messages, voice mails, and IMs eventually get ignored themselves. Dream Girls understand that, which is why they know it's respectful to let a guy know they got his message as soon as they can, without being rude to someone they are with in person of course.

GUYS DON'T NEED NO STINKIN' BADGERING

Now let's say the shoe is on the other foot. What if you sent a text message to your guy, only he didn't get back to you? Feelings of ostracism being what they are, you start to have crazy thoughts. You wonder what he's doing that's so important that he can't stop for two seconds to send you a lousy text. So you send another one ... and another one ... and still another one, until he finally messages you back.

If this is you—and I hope it isn't—you seriously need to stop this. Right away.

Surveillance messaging, or *badgering*, is not just annoying, it can destroy all types of relationships. Like we said before, you do not have a right to know what your guy is doing or where he's going or who he's with 24/7 any more than he has a right to know that about you. Go back to the final question we raised at the beginning of the chapter:

Do guys trust girls who continually check up on them with calls or texts?

Here's the answer: No. Relationships are built on trust. That means giving each other a little space. That means giving each other the benefit of the doubt.

Now it's one thing if you have reason to believe he's not replying to you because he's doing something he shouldn't be doing, like cheating on you. That's when you talk to him and find out what's going on.

But if it's nothing like that at all, and it's a matter of he didn't get back to you right away because *he* was at the movies or a wedding or an area where he couldn't receive a signal or someplace else where using a cell phone simply wasn't appropriate, then maybe it's time for you to start working out your own issues of trust. Guys don't like surveillance messaging. It's a form of mistreatment (not to mention, mistrust) that they really, really resent. Take it from the guys themselves:

))) What Guys Are Saying About Surveillance Texting

This one girl sent me a text message every ten minutes. She always wanted to know who I was with, what I was doing, when I was going to be done with my friends and come to see her. She pissed me off. She even texted me in the middle of the night to see if I was home and asleep! I repeat—she woke me up to ask me if I was sleeping. How stupid is that?
　　—Steve, USA

My ex-girlfriend called me all day to ask me stuff. She wanted to know where I was or what I was doing. She said she just loved me so much, she wanted to know what was going on with me. I felt she didn't trust me or that she was way too needy. We broke up because I stopped answering all her calls. She was psycho!
—Shane, USA

GUYS DON'T NEED NO STINKIN' BULLYING EITHER

Typically we think of guys as bullies. But girls can be bullies, too, especially in the world of online communications. Bullying through messaging is on the rise; and, believe me, I've refereed enough of these squabbles to know that girls do their share, too. A recent study done by Clemson University revealed that girls are almost twice as likely as boys are to bully or be bullied through the Internet or by cell phone. Jessica Reeves reveals in an article in the *Chicago Tribune* that the US Justice Department found that girls are the perpetrators for 61 percent of in-person bullying. In the past few years, physical assault perpetrated by girls is up by over a whopping 40 percent.

Bullying is mean, and it harms people. Megan Meier, a thirteen-year-old girl, committed suicide after being taunted on MySpace. Dream Girls don't message threatening or cruel comments to guys or girls, and they certainly don't post a comment in a public forum to start a fight within a virtual social network—period.

It's easy to let yourself get carried away when you are online or texting. Something mysterious happens when you sit in front of a computer screen or hold a cell phone in your hand, ready to type a message. You become bolder, more brazen. You feel you can write whatever you really want to say because the person receiving your message may be miles and miles away, or close but still out of touch so you don't have to deal with the consequences of your communication.

Did you ever see the movie *The Mask*? Jim Carrey's character put the wooden mask to his face, and, wow, all of his inner desires that he'd kept under wraps in the real world immediately came out. What happens to you when you're online is sort of like what happened to the character Carrey played in the movie. Those inner voices that you keep to yourself suddenly come to life behind the safety of the screen. So you can type, "I have the biggest crush on you!" and not have to deal with seeing the look on a guy's face when he learns you are smitten with him. Or you can type, "You are an idiot and should just die!" because you know you can't get punched in the face when the person reading your message isn't face-to-face with you.

I have heard stories from my MySpace friends telling me how girls fight and leave nasty comments on other people's profiles. Of course, the friends of the girls involved jumped into the fray and, suddenly, a whole community of people were fighting amongst each other.

Dream Girls keep their disagreements to themselves. That means the answer to whether leaving mean comments on someone's MySpace or Facebook profile lowers your trustworthiness is a resounding *yes.*

Guys don't like it when girls write mean things to anyone. A public forum is no place for a catfight or lover's quarrel. If a girl is capable of leaving nasty comments to other people, a guy will wonder what she is capable of writing about *him* if he should ever upset her. Girls who are willing to air their dirty laundry in public have less respect from guys. They certainly aren't Dream Girls.

"But, Dr. Jenn, what if someone writes something mean and nasty on my comment page?"

Well, first of all, go into your profile and delete it right away. Then take a deep breath, count to ten (really, it helps!), think about Gwen Stefani's advice ("I ain't no holla back girl"), and let it go.

If you do have a beef with someone online, do the rest of the group a favor *and keep it between yourselves.* Life is complicated enough without adding more drama on MySpace, Facebook, chat rooms, or any other online forums. If you insist on carrying on, do it privately.

Of course, it goes without saying that Dream Girls don't bully anyone in person. But we'll say it anyway just so we know everyone got the memo. Bullies aren't just using the Internet or using cell phones to harass their victims. They get right in your face and go to work. But no girl who wants to win the love and respect of a guy would bully anyone in any way. If a girl is angry with someone, she will use all of her detective listening skills to solve the problem. Right? *Right!*

Okay. So you didn't take your fight public. Instead, you sent the person you were angry with a no-holds-barred message, the kind you would never have the guts to say face-to-face. Is it okay for you do that? Do guys trust girls who snap people's heads off in a text, email or voice message?

No, they don't. Guys respect girls who practice detective listening, and detective listeners remain calm and try to understand other people, even when they are angry. Detective listening isn't just for when you are face-to-face with another person. It's for all types of communication.

Guys trust girls who use respectful communication at all times. It's just that simple. If you want to earn a guy's respect, you must let him know that you not only deserve his respect, but will be a respectful member of his safe tribe and treat him and the other tribal members with respect. That also means you will show yourself respect as well.

To sum up the issues concerning trust and new communications technology, Dream Girls ask themselves these questions *before* their fingers hit the keyboard:

- Are the words I'm about to write words I would say to this person if we were standing face-to-face?
- How will the other person feel once he or she sees what I've written?
- How will the other person feel about what I have written about him or her?
- How would I feel if this were written about me?
- Am I simply hiding behind the safety of a screen?
- Will what I have written cause our group of friends to pick sides?
- Would I trust a person who was going to write what I want to write?
- Will I end up looking like a just-in-his-jeans girl or a Dream Girl?

Dream Girls know that lashing out at someone by typing a nasty message or comment is something that rarely works to solve problems.

what guys want you to know:

Guys want girls to use electronic communication respectfully.

Secret No. 20

Blogs and other interactive sites like YouTube, where users are invited to post comments, have also become breeding grounds for meanness. Have you ever stopped to read some of the comments people leave about each other on places like YouTube? Many of the comments are derogatory.

Sure, you and I both know that a lot of what we see on YouTube or any other place where uploads are available is just plain silly. But that doesn't mean we don't appreciate the time and energy it took to create and share those videos or blogs. If you don't like what you see, go look for something else. What's the point in attacking the person who put it there? Just because you didn't care for the video or blog doesn't mean nobody else will. The old saying "If you don't have anything nice to say, don't say anything at all," is still a good saying for today.

Girls who hide behind the safety of a screen in order to be mean and nasty aren't the type of girl that a guy wants to build a solid, trusting relationship with.

EMERGENCY ROOM PROCEDURES FOR LIARS, CHEATERS, AND CHRONIC MISTREATERS

Okay, so you've lied to your previous boyfriends or perhaps even cheated on them. You've broken their hearts, upset them, bullied them, badgered them, hijacked their passwords or passed them on to others, flamed them with a public comment, and done just about everything else you can do to wreck your chances at being a Dream Girl. Your reputation is toast. You've got a scarlet letter branded on your forehead that guys can see from miles away: This girl is damaged goods. You can't trust her. She's not worthy of being loved. She's not worthy of a long-term relationship. .

What do you do? What *can* you do? Is there even hope for you? Is it still possible to become a Dream Girl, no matter how badly you've screwed things up before?

Sure, it's possible. It's *always* possible. That's part of the beauty of being human. It's always possible to improve. It's always possible to change our behavior, if we're willing to do the work.

True, given how badly you've hurt people in the past, the damage to your reputation is pretty severe. We're talking major bleeding here, and possibly even surgery. You're going to need a little help before you're whole again.

Fortunately, there's a place you can go, no matter how critical your condition. I call it the R-ER: reputation emergency room.

If you were experiencing a physical emergency, the doctors and nurses would do all they could to deal with the worst, life-threatening damage; then they would work on the smaller injuries. After all, it does no good to set your broken arm when you're bleeding to death. It's just the opposite in the R-ER. You start with the small things and work your way up to the major things. The great thing about the R-ER is that it begins with you. All the tools you need to heal your wounded soul are right inside you. You don't have to have a bunch of people hovering over you, helping you.

Make a list of all the things you've done to damage other people's feelings. Begin with the little stuff, the relatively minor infractions; then work your way up to the capital offenses—the really rotten things you've done. Then start making amends.

> **DR. JENN SAYS...**
>
> *If you've lied and cheated and want to repair the damage to your reputation, check yourself into the R-ER.*

Maybe you need to return that book you borrowed from Jim that you never gave back. Maybe you need to apologize to Jane for the hurtful name you called her online under the guise of another username or your own. Maybe you need to gather all your friends together and make an announcement—kind of like an intervention, only you're the one intervening to them ... *on behalf of yourself.* Tell them that you want to be a better friend to them in the future and that you're working on things to help you do that. Ask them for their patience and, above all, ask for their forgiveness. Then make sure you forgive yourself! That's just as important.

Whatever you need to do to make amends for the hurt you've caused in the past, *do it in person* if you possibly can. Yes, e-mails, IMs, text messages, or comments left on MySpace profiles are a lot more convenient; but remember, this is not about what's convenient to you. It is about what's important to the people you care about.

Dream Girls know that when it comes to delicate communications, be it a heartfelt apology or a declaration of love, our words will mean so much more when they come from us, face-to-face. That's the sort of thing that can build your trust account back to where it was before.

Bonus Secret

Even the most untrustworthy girl can earn back her trust with guys. It takes time and effort, but you can do it. Even better, guys want you to earn back their trust. They are rooting for you. So if you really want to make amends and become a Dream Girl, say goodbye to being a just-in-his-jeans girl. It's worth going for!

Here are some of the differences between Dream Girls and just-in-his-jeans girls when it comes to trust. I have left some blank spots for you to fill in what you remember from this chapter or any thoughts you'd like to add concerning trust and new communications technology.

DREAM GIRLS	JUST-IN-HIS-JEANS GIRLS
• Know that trust issues include understanding to how to use new communications technology respectfully	• Believe that as long as they don't lie and cheat, they are doing all they can to win a guy's respect
• Watch what they type in any type of message	• Fire off whatever they want to say with no thought about its effect on someone
• Don't badger their friends about where they are every minute of the day	• Need to know where people are all the time and call or text to keep track of everyone
• Don't flirt via text, IMs, or other communications devices with other guys when they are in a relationship	• Flirt with other guys and draw attention to themselves when they are in a relationship
• Know that guys want their respect	• Do not understand about giving respect to get respect
• Keep their "fights" private	• Make their fights public
• Understand that if they mess up, they can still become a Dream Girl	• Give up if they screw up without trying to better themselves
• Know that trust is fragile and treats it with care	• Believe that trust can survive the worst of betrayals

Dream Girls-in-training know that there is a lot to learn about gaining love and respect. They are willing to learn the new issues about trust in today's technological world, but they're also willing to learn about some of the "old-fashioned" things that can get in the way of showing a guy respect, such as nagging, gossiping, and mothering. We'll be covering these and other topics in the next chapter, so sharpen your pencils and take notes. There might just be a quiz!

BONUS INFO FROM DR. JENN

Today's new communications technology is amazing. We are now capable of sharing large amounts of information with each other. It has made the world smaller in that we can communicate with people from all over the globe quickly and easily. However, like just about everything else these days, new technology comes with a price—and I'm not talking about the numbers you see on a tag.

One of the prices we pay for our attachment to our new "toys" is that it can be easy to forget how to communicate in person, face-to-face. Or worse, we forget that we even *need* to see people face-to-face. We are slowly beginning to lose our respect and empathy for other people. It's just a small crack in our humanity, but it grows every day.

So with that in mind, I encourage you to:

1) Set limits on your computer or cell phone use (such as, don't sleep with your cell phone or your instant messenger on) and let your friends know your limits. Get a full night's sleep without the noise of a machine going off every time someone wants to reach you.

2) Make sure you take time to hang out with friends in person and have fun.

3) Don't use your computer or cell phone to try to communicate how you *feel* about anything important. People need to either *hear* you or *see* you in order for the mirror neurons in their brains to fire. Those neurons are part of what help us remain human and empathic.

4) Don't use your computer or cell phone to spread gossip, rumors, or nasty remarks about anyone.

5) If you feel threatened by anyone via a message of any kind, and you are truly scared, let an adult or the police know.

Love Doesn't Look Like This

"Stop all the nagging crap. I mean, really. You aren't my mom. Stop being such a gossip and a bitch to people and please get a grip on your jealousy. Treat people the way you want them to treat you!"
—Louis, USA

Dream Girls-in-waiting, let's do a quick review. You have learned that self-respect, detective listening, and being trustworthy gets you respect and affection. Now let's add a lesson about what love looks like—or, as Louis shows us in his words above, what love *doesn't* look like.

Love is not about gossiping, nagging, mothering, or other forms of mistreatment. Showing love to others will get you love and respect in return.

Of course, there's no guarantee that the guy you are dying to be with will feel the same *type* of attraction or affection toward you. That sort of attraction has other elements in it that no book can teach you. None of us fully understands why people are sexually or romantically pulled toward one person and not another.

But certainly, respect, listening, and trust are all major ingredients that will make you attractive to other people, whether as a potential relationship partner or simply as a friend. Add showing love to what you've already learned, and you'll make yourself even more attractive. And the best way any of us can show love is to understand what love means.

Love, in the true purest sense of the word, is *the act of good toward others*. I'm not talking about the Hollywood movie version of love, which is infatuation, lots of sex, and a happy ending two hours later. Nor am I talking about love as that spine-tingling feeling you have for your new crush or the rush of pleasure you get from being around people you care about. No, I'm simply talking about *acting* for the good of all others. In other words, I'm talking about love as an action you do—a choice you can make. I'm talking about love as your *attitude* and *behavior* toward other people, not how you feel about them.

"Come on, Dr. Jenn, love is a choice? I can't love bitchy girls or guys who are jerks."

Yeah, it's kinda confusing, isn't it? I'm not saying you have to have feelings of love for them, but you do have to act lovingly towards them.

The secret about love in action is that, when you show love to people, no matter what you feel toward them or how they might feel toward you, eventually you'll grow more and more *capable* of feeling love for the people you're acting lovingly toward—or for that matter, anyone else.

That's why the quote from Louis is a good starting point for our discussion. Gossiping, bitching people out, and the other forms of mistreatments we're about to explore are all repulsive behaviors—quite literally, behaviors that make us unattractive, behaviors that repel others from us. The better we understand the things that make us unattractive, the greater capacity we'll have for acting and behaving in a kind, loving way that will attract others to us.

That's what it's all about, ladies. I am asking you, as Dream Girls in the making, to go the extra distance and remember that love is no different than the golden rule: it asks us to treat others as you want them to treat you.

Let me repeat that, because it's an idea that's important not only to this chapter but, indeed, this entire book. Treat others as you want them to treat you.

Sure, that sounds corny, but wait till you see what happens once you know what love looks like.

When you resist the urge to bitch someone out or talk smack about them or overly control their life—and instead treat them in a way that shows them just how great your capacity for love is—it places the Dream Girl crown more securely on your head. You can't possibly be mistaken for a just-in-his-jeans girl when you're sporting all those jewels.

"There you go again, Dr. Jenn, with that all Dream Girl crown jewels stuff!"

Yep, that's right. And you want to know why? Dream Girls really are like royalty—not royalty in the sense of having others bow down to you or curtsey or any of that I'm-better-than-you stuff, but royalty in the sense that Dream Girls are *rare*. They don't blindly follow what other girls are doing just to fit in. Rather, Dream Girls try to live their lives in a way that shows love in action even if it's not the cool thing to do. They not only want to touch the lives of other people but to make the lives of other people better. Not everyone's willing to do that, but that's what makes Dream Girls special.

THE 411 ABOUT GOSSIP

We live in a voyeuristic society that loves to gobble up information about the lives of famous people—the juicier, the better. It's one of the reasons why YouTube, MySpace and Facebook have become so popular. Magazines like *InStyle* and *Us Weekly*; tabloids like *The Globe, The Star*, and *The National Enquirer*; television shows like *The Insiders* and *Access Hollywood*; and Web sites and blogs like TMZ.com and PerezHilton.com make big bank providing the dirt on celebrities, whether they're movie stars, music stars, athletes, politicians, power brokers, or other members of the rich and famous. The more scandalous the news, the more money these media outlets make bringing it to the public.

And it's not just about money either. Whether she was sniping at Donald Trump or sparring with Elizabeth Hasselback, a few years back,

Rosie O'Donnell was one of the best things that ever happened to *The View* in terms of ratings, which went up 15 percent during Rosie's year on the show. Message boards, blogs, cable television, and other gossip hounds couldn't wait to report on whatever outrageous thing she was going to say next.

Gossip is so accepted in our culture, we usually don't think twice when we gossip about others. Why should we? It certainly seems no one else is keeping their hands over their mouths and staying quiet.

Sure, sometimes gossip can be fairly innocent. After all, it's just another way to share information about others. We've all heard our friends talk about someone else, and it's not always backstabbing, judgmental, or mean. You know, stuff like, "Did you hear Hallie got a brand new Prius because her mom loved Al Gore's movie, *An Inconvenient Truth?*" Or "John got a kitten and didn't tell his dad." Or "Jo Jo is moving this fall back to Eagle County." Any one of those sentences could be the start of a gossip fest, or any other conversation, for that matter, that is most likely fairly harmless. It's just neutral information sharing.

But gossip can also be cruel. What if the talk about Hallie and her Prius was focused around the idea that Hallie was a spoiled little brat for getting a new car? What if the idea was to make John look like a dumbass for trying to sneak a new pet into the house? What if someone whispered that Jo Jo was moving to stay with an aunt because she is pregnant and her parents want her away from the baby's father and, by the way, how could she be so careless to get pregnant in the first place?

It's all too easy to shift gears from neutral information sharing and into full-throttle story sharing that will eventually result in someone passing judgment on another person. Gossip humiliates and can destroy not only someone else's reputation but your reputation as well. Gossip is like a boomerang: it has a long reach to hurt others, and it heads straight back to smack you upside the head with an enormous ouch to your reputation. The more you gossip, the more guys realize you aren't respectful of yourself, aren't showing love to other people, and aren't living by the golden rule.

Guys don't like it when you gossip in ways that hurt others. If you're so willing to pass judgment on other people, guys wonder what you might say about them. In other words, if you can be so unloving towards others, why would a guy assume you'd always be loving towards him?

DON'T LOWER YOURSELF TO GOSSIP'S LEVEL

Some girls gossip to make others look small, but in fact the opposite happens. When you gossip, you lower yourself to the level of a just-in-his-jeans girl, which is certainly not a place you want to be if you ultimately want to be loved.

In a way, gossip is no different than alcohol, recreational drugs, or any other habit that can turn destructive at the first sign of abuse. Once you experience that first "high" of judging everyone and spreading rumors about people, you lose perspective over who and what you are. You start manipulating people, setting them up for a fall so you can get off on their misery. You begin looking down on others, while thinking you are better. Before you realize it, you begin to feel as if everyone needs to live up to what *you* believe is true, while conveniently forgetting *there are six billion other people on the planet* who may not agree with you.

No one is less than you; nor is anyone above you. All six billion of us are doing our best with the wounds we have and the tools at our disposal. Dream Girls know that. That's why they strive to lend others a helping hand, a compassionate ear, or feelings of empathy, rather than gossip about others.

DR. JENN SAYS...

Gossiping hurts you and others!

There are many types of gossip. Some gossip makes us feel better when others feel pain, while some gossip is an act of revenge. Let's look at some of the different kinds of gossip so you can figure out which type you do more than others. We'll also look at some ways you can curb your "gossip fix" so that you won't end up looking like a just-in-his-jeans girl.

GLOWING AND CROWING OVER PEOPLE'S PAIN

We like to take pleasure in the misery of others, especially the misery of celebrities. There's a word for that; it's called *schadenfreude.* It's a German word, but the activity has become uniquely American.

Remember back when the headlines were all about Paris doing something stupid, Lindsay's sobriety challenges, Amy Winehouse's refusal to go to rehab, or another meltdown by Britney? The whole world watched and just shook their heads over these ladies.

Watching celebrities disgrace themselves or make bad decisions are things we really enjoy. Maybe we take comfort in knowing that even famous people are still capable of doing the same stupid things we do. Maybe we just like to build people up in order to see them fall. Whatever the reason, everyone seems to get a kick out of the misfortunes of famous people, and the world tends to feast most aggressively on female celebrities' misfortunes and mistakes.

Of course, sometimes we take pleasure in the misery of ordinary people, especially people who have been mean to us or have hurt us in other ways, or who we simply do not like. It somehow justifies our feelings. We can point our finger and say, "Ha-ha—karma!" We feel the person got what was coming to him or her.

what guys want you to know:

Guys don't value girls who take pleasure in the pain of others.

Secret No. 21

Jessica sure took pleasure in the misery of her best friend named Scott. She and Scott did everything together their senior year of high school. A week before graduation, Scott met Jessica's archenemy, Cathy. Jessica had fought with Cathy the year before over a guy, and Jessica had never forgiven her for it. Scott was excited that a new girl had come into his life and that she had an attraction for him. He began to spend more time with Cathy than he did with Jessica. That made sense, because Cathy was slowly becoming Scott's girlfriend. Jessica was afraid of losing her best friend, so she started gossiping about Cathy. As she confessed to me:

> Dr. Jenn, I said some really cruel and ugly things about Cathy. I talked so much smack about her being a slut and a bitch. I lost Scott's friendship. I pushed him away with my big mouth.

Scott and Cathy ended up living together, and eventually they got engaged. Though Jessica had lost touch with Scott, she heard through a friend that Scott and Cathy's relationship ended badly after a few years—*really badly*. But instead of trying to rekindle her friendship with Scott or at least trying to show him compassion and help him back up on his feet, Jessica lowered herself down to the level of the gossip vineyard.

> I basked in his misery because I felt like I'd been proven right after all. I got to gloat and tell everyone that he should have listened to me in the beginning when we were in high school. I trashed Cathy even more, not once thinking about what kind of pain she or Scott might have been in. I just felt so damn ... right. And since they had finally broken up, I figured Scott got what was coming to him.
>
> Wow, how small I was for thinking that.
>
> A friend should always be there for a friend. But I was immature; I was glowing and crowing over Scott's misery. I may not have liked Cathy, but he did. He loved her and wanted to marry her. I hurt my relationship with him because I gossiped about her and him all the time. I wanted to be right more than I wanted to be of help.

Jessica cried as she told me her story. As we all know, sometimes it hurts to realize just how ugly we can be to each other. But sometimes life gives us a second chance:

> I look back now and wonder how we were able to salvage our friendship ... but we did.

*I apologized to Scott, and he told me that my gossiping
pushed him away. He said that, if I'd have sat down with him
when he first met Cathy and talked to him about my fears
about her, and listened to his side of the story, we might have
been able to avoid so much pain in our relationship with each
other. It was never my place to tell him who he could or could
not date, let alone gossip so cruelly about the two of them,
especially after they broke up.*

Jessica and Scott are good friends now, but it didn't happen overnight. It took years before they could get back to the level of friendship
they had before, just as it takes time for any two people to rebuild a
broken trust.

Jessica's story is a good example of
what love doesn't look like. Had she been
able to show Cathy love by keeping her
own mouth shut and not gossiping about
her, a lot of pain and drama could have
been avoided. That's not to say that Scott
and Cathy would have worked out as a
couple; as it happened, they had their
own issues. But think how much bigger a person Jessica would have
been had she not spread her judgments about Cathy and Scott through
the gossip grapevine.

> **DR. JENN SAYS...**
>
> *Showing love in action is
> often as simple as keeping
> your mouth shut.*

To stop gloating over someone else's pain, remember that he or she
is human and that you owe it to that person as a fellow human being to
recognize him or her as such. You may not like the person, but you can
still show him or her compassion, rather than causing even more pain
by gossiping about his or her plight.

Remember the point we made at the end of Chapter Three: If you
can't say anything nice, don't say anything at all.

GOSSIP AS A POUND OF FLESH

Some girls gossip about others to level the score, to get back at someone they think has slighted them in some way. Rather than use their detective listening skills to get to the bottom of the conflict and resolve it peacefully, they spread nasty rumors as their weapons of choice. Janet's story shows how gossip hurts others and how it hurt her as well.

Janet started gossiping about a couple of girls she didn't like when she was in ninth grade. Apparently, one of the girls had slighted her in some way, and by junior year, the feud escalated. Janet was out for blood; she kept her ears open for any juicy tidbit she could use about either one of the girls. Like Shylock in Shakespeare's *The Merchant of Venice*, she wanted her pound of flesh.

One day, Janet heard a rumor that one of the girls may have contracted herpes. Janet didn't care whether it was true or not; all she saw was her opportunity, and boy, did she run with it! She spread that rumor like jelly on toast, real smooth and easy. Not only did she talk to people about the girl, she texted *and* sent messages to people's Facebook accounts, ensuring the rumor would spread far and wide. She just wanted to cause the girl pain.

When you act deliberately mean like that, you've entangled yourself in the gossip vineyard, stomping sour grapes that make you unpalatable to people. And sure enough, Janet lost friends by gossiping. Not only were her girlfriends afraid she'd spread lies about them if they upset her, but once guys found out what she had done, they wanted no part of her, either. A girl who spreads false rumors, a girl who chooses to hurt others on purpose, is no one's idea of a Dream Girl.

what guys want you to know:

Guys don't respect or trust girls who gossip because gossiping is not love in action. Guys show more love and respect to girls who know how to show love and respect.

Secret No. 22

What makes Janet's story really sad is that, aside from her vendetta with these two girls, she was actually a really good kid. She valued honesty, integrity, trust, truth, compassion, and many other noble ideals. The problem was, she wasn't living her values. She may have seen herself as a Dream Girl, but her actions made her look like a just-in-his-jeans girl. Remember the exercise in Chapter One where you sent out an "invitation" for others to recognize your values? Next time you think about spreading a rumor about someone you don't like, ask yourself the following questions before you take revenge:

> *How do other people see me? Is this the kind of behavior I want to invite others to think I value?*
>
> *Are my actions consistent with the values I want to uphold?*
>
> *If they're not consistent, what do I need to do to get back on track and live according to my values?*
>
> *Are my actions love in action? Am I treating someone the way I want to be treated?*

Dream Girls know that gossiping is no way to show love to anyone. They know that even if they don't like someone, they can still show love by treating others kindly and following the golden rule.

GOSSIPING ABOUT YOUR SEX LIFE

It used to be that guys were the ones who engaged in "locker room talk"—you know, bragging to their buddies whenever possible about their latest sexual conquests. Not anymore. Nowadays, it's girls who are more likely to spill the beans about their love lives, sharing every gory detail with all of their girlfriends.

Guys don't respect girls who kiss and tell. Every time you cup your hand to your mouth, whisper into a friend's ear, and gossip about your sexual secrets, you can bet those secrets won't stay that way for long. Maybe your antics won't show up on YouTube or share shelf space next to the sexcapades DVDs of Pamela or Paris, but, as far as your reputation goes, once the news of your exploits is broadcast to your other friends, they might as well be.

That's essentially what happened to Gina, an eighteen-year-old from California. Gina's a nice, well-meaning girl, who learned the hard way what gossip can do to an otherwise good reputation.

Gina dated a guy she really liked. He didn't want a long-term relationship, but she was okay with that. The trouble was, she gossiped about him and his lack-of-commitment issues with some of her girlfriends. Not only that, she shared some of their most intimate moments.

Gina's friends swore to take the conversation to their graves. But of course, they were still alive and kicking when the conversation got back to the guy Gina was dating. He freaked out! In fact, he was so upset, he laced up his running shoes faster than you can say "break up."

Poor Gina. She didn't even get to have a short-term relationship. Her reputation as a respectful, trustworthy person was shot to pieces. She regrets what she did and vows next time to keep her mouth shut.

Gina's gossip was self-serving: it made her feel proud to share her sexual exploits. That's what happens when you share bedroom secrets with your friends. You are comparing notes, showing off what you know, and not keeping your intimate details, well, intimate. Gina may have gratified herself, so to speak, but it obviously came at a price. By serving her own needs without any consideration for the needs of her romantic partner, she lost his trust, which, as we know, is the one thing on which all lasting relationships are built.

So how do you stop from gossiping about your sex life? Imagine your guy is standing next to you. If you wouldn't say something with him standing there, then don't say it, even though he isn't there. Either that, or try changing the subject. Then switch into detective listening mode and turn the spotlight on the people who you are talking with. Find out more things about them, provided it isn't details about *their* sex life. They will appreciate the attention and will respect you for keeping your private life private.

GOSSIP AS A CONNECTOR

Girls also gossip as a way to feel connected. When a group of girls are together and talking about people who aren't part of the group, the bond among the girls within the group suddenly feels tighter. It's like it's "us against them." The problem is that the person (or people) you are talking about becomes an "enemy image." Then it's all too easy to dismiss them and be cruel to them.

The concept of an enemy image comes from a clinical psychologist named Marshall Rosenberg. He started the Center for Nonviolent Communication after growing up in a rough neighborhood in Detroit. Rosenberg developed a way of communicating with people as part of his efforts to reduce violence. In essence, he believes that when you belittle others in your talking, you no longer see them as human beings but, instead, as simply "things." When we reduce people to things, they become an enemy image in our eyes.

When you use gossip as a divisive tool, you create not only an enemy image but actual enemies for yourself. That's what happened to Janet after she told people that the girl she didn't like had herpes. Other girls were afraid she'd gossip about them. That's also what happens to girls who bully or talk smack about others in general, whether in person or online.

what guys want you to know:

Guys don't like it when you and your friends gossip about other people. They want you to find healthier ways to feel connected. Secret No. 23

Okay, so you like hanging out with your friends and gossiping about all the girls and guys you don't like for one reason or another. You're not hurting anyone; it's just you and your safe tribe chilling, connecting, and doing stuff together. You are united, even if the only thing you really have in common is your dislike of the same people. And besides, you and your posse are tight—what's said in the tribe, stays in the tribe, right? Where's the harm in that?

This is a tough one, girls, because here we're talking about a kind of peer pressure. And we all know how difficult peer pressure can be to overcome.

There may come a time when you understand gossip is hurtful and you don't want to participate. The problem is, everyone else in your group still thinks it's okay. Suddenly, you're the minority voice, but you don't want to be seen as an outcast and tell everyone to shut up. What do you do?

The answer is really simple. Change the topic of conversation. This is one time when it's okay to switch the conversation. Jump in and get your friends talking about something else if you can.

Sarah, an eighteen-year-old Dream Girl, told me that she gets her friends to stop gossiping about others by saying, "Sure glad we don't have her (or his) life." Then she changes the topic. She said, "I mean it in a compassionate way. I really *am* glad I don't have the drama or the troubles that the person we are gossiping about has." She added that she has a remarkable success rate of changing the topic whenever she uses that statement, and the gossiping stops.

USING GOSSIP TO AVOID CONFRONTATION

Girls also gossip to win sympathy or understanding from their friends, especially after they've been hurt by other people. You understand why: our friends are our friends. They pick us up when we feel down. Once we tell them about the nasty thing Sally did to us, we can count on our friends to make us feel better by saying something nasty about her. Besides, it's way easier to talk trash about Sally with our friends than to confront her face-to-face and deal with the issue head on. When you turn to another person to air your gripes about what someone else has done to you, you create a *triangle relationship*.

The problem with most triangle relationships is that the person you drag into your drama doesn't need to be there. The person who needs to be there, of course, is the one you have the beef with. Hey, no one can blame you if you hate confrontation; so does almost everyone else. After all, it's not easy and often takes a lot of courage to talk rationally with people who have upset us. We're either afraid of how they're going to react, or we are so pissed off that we can't think straight, so we put it off altogether.

The problem is, the conflict you have with the other person isn't going to resolve itself unless you tell that person about it. That's why the direct approach is always the best.

Now if you're worried about what the person might say or how you might react, don't sweat it; this is where your detective listening skills can once again pull you through. Tell your side of the story as simply as you can, then listen to the person's response. You may not agree with what he or she has to say (and let's face it, if the person's upset you, you probably won't), but at least you listened to him or her ... and, hopefully, he or she has listened to you. Now that you've gotten things out into the open, you've made it possible for you both to move on with your lives without dragging anyone else into it.

Whenever you talk about someone who is not there with you and share facts or rumors about them that could be hurtful, know that you're about to step into the gossip vineyard *and tell yourself to stop.* Tell whoever you are talking to that you realize what you are saying isn't kind, then apologize and change the subject. It's not always easy, but it's a big step to becoming a Dream Girl.

Guys appreciate girls who don't spread nasty rumors and gossip about others. Learning to keep your gossiping under control now will help you in the adult world when you get there.

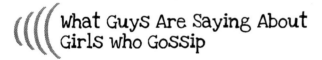

What Guys Are Saying About Girls who Gossip

Shut up and be nice. Everyone gossips to an extent, but when you bitch, bitch, bitch, it is annoying and a total turnoff.
   —Nicholas, USA

When a girl gossips, it undermines my trust and confidence in what I can tell her, because she is probably going to blab it to someone else. It is very, very important to me to be able to trust my girlfriend.
   —Erik, Egypt

Gossiping about other people isn't right. I have been talked about, and it hurts.
  —Ryan, Australia

Gossiping is retarded! The only reason people gossip is because their own life is way too boring, and they have to bring someone else down in order to raise themselves up. Gossip lowers my respect for a girl.
  —Shannon, USA

If I find out a girl has been doing this [gossiping] to my mutual friends (as happened recently), I lose most, if not all attraction for them. I have high standards, especially when it comes to this sort of thing (trust, etc.), so something like this really annoys me.
  —Dylan, USA

Gossip is boring. Who really cares about who is going out with who, like anyone really needs to know unless it involves them in some way. It's a waste of time, and, girls, it's really annoying.
  —Tim, Australia

Gossiping shows a personality flaw, and it lessens my respect.
  —Jacob, USA

I would expect the girl not to gossip to mutual friends, just the same as I would do for anyone. I don't appreciate being talked about behind my back, which is why I don't do it to any of my friends.
  —Mike, USA

Girls, shut up! You talk too much shit about nothing. So many girls I know bitch about everything; just makes you wonder

what they say about you.
—Aaron, Australia

Gossiping isn't good! Girls, never be a two-faced, backstabbing friend.
—Marco, Mexico

Teenage girls gossip too much. It causes too many problems, and I think it needs to stop.
—Travis, USA

DISS AND BE DISMISSED

Remember, ladies, dissing is short for "disrespect"; and we all know how important respect and self-respect are when it comes to reaching Dream Girl status.

When you diss on people behind their backs, of course, you show a lack of respect for others, not to mention a lack of respect for yourself. Not only that, because you've dissed on others in front of a guy without taking anything else into consideration—like the possibility *he may actually know and like* some of the people you've just dissed or *may be offended* by that kind of negative talk in the first place—you've also managed to demonstrate a lack of respect for him. That's quite a triple axel you've just pulled off. No wonder so many girls who are into dissing get dismissed by a lot of guys.

Dissing is a form of putting down our friends, family, possessions, and even ourselves that can be as destructive as it is vicious. Dissing is similar to gossip in that it (1) usually concerns other people, (2) is often mean, and (3) can mess up your chances of becoming a Dream Girl.

Gossiping is sharing information about people that may or may not be based on facts. For example, "Maddie cut her hair just like Liz's because Maddie is afraid her boyfriend might be interested in Liz, and I think he is going to dump Maddie." Now, we have no idea whether or not the current state of Maddie's love life has anything to do with her decision to have her hair done just like Liz's. For all we know, Maddie may have seen the same photo in *Vogue* or *Cosmo* that Liz saw before Liz got her hair done last week. But if you like to gossip, that doesn't matter. People who like to gossip just want to share the story.

Dissing, on the other hand, is a quick put-down we make based entirely on our opinion, as in, "Maddie's such an idiot for cutting her hair like that."

Sometimes the difference between gossiping and dissing can be a fine line, so don't worry if you confuse the two. The thing to remember is this: dissing is no more an example of love in action than gossiping is. Love in action is showing compassion and empathy for others, not passing judgment on them.

We all know girls who feel their opinion is warranted no matter what the subject is; they believe that they're welcome to share that opinion regardless of the circumstances. They feel they need to tell a guy just what they think of his best friend or the crowd he hangs with or the other girls he's seen. It doesn't matter to her whether he's known his best friend since kindergarten or just met him last year; if she doesn't like his best friend or thinks he's somehow "wrong" for him, she won't think twice about saying so. After all, *it's her opinion, damn it*, and she's entitled to it.

A girl like that assumes that guys either (1) find dissing about others to be attractive or (2) will overlook her tendency to diss if they don't find it attractive. But here's the deal: they don't and they won't.

What do guys consider dissing? Try putting down your friends, putting down his friends, putting down your parents or relatives (or his), putting down people you or he work with, putting down people you don't even know. In other words, dissing includes just about any comment you can make about yourself or someone else that is negative or judgmental.

Most people put down others in order to build themselves up. But as we've seen before, the opposite usually happens. Just as gossip makes us look smaller, so does dissing other people. In addition, dissing makes us look less trustworthy, especially in the eyes of a guy. After all, if you're so willing to trash others in front of him, he can only imagine what you're going to say about *him* in front of other people.

Guys also hate it when girls diss themselves. Why? Because they have no idea what to say in return.

Think about it. If you're a guy and you're with a girl who constantly says she's too fat or too short or too flat or whatever she likes to say to put herself down, what are you supposed to think: is she fishing for a compliment or looking for sympathy, or does she really feel that way about herself? If that's how she really feels about herself, does she want you to validate it or try to make her feel better?

If you say, "Gee, you're right, you *are* fat," you can bet she'll respond with, "How can you possibly say that?" You'll spend the rest of the evening apologizing for being so insensitive. That's a real mood killer.

On the other hand, you could say, "It's okay, don't be so hard on yourself," but, because she's so into self-loathing, she's likely to instigate a fight. Either way, you can't win.

That's why guys stay clear of girls who diss themselves. Dealing with their self-dissing is way too confusing, and ultimately not worth the hassle.

what guys want you to know:

Guys don't appreciate girls who diss on their friends or family. They especially hate it when girls diss on themselves.

Secret No. 24

To illustrate how dissing can make an otherwise attractive, good-hearted, well-meaning would-be Dream Girl look unattractive in the eyes of other people, let me tell you about a girl named Alyson. Alyson grew up in a dysfunctional household where she felt she didn't matter very much. She felt that people she met would be just like her family and blow her off. She was so worried about fitting in and making herself look good to people, she often put down others, thinking for some reason that it would make her seem bigger, better, and brighter than she actually was and that the guy she liked would therefore like her.

This, of course, is a classic example of someone using dissing to compensate for a deep-seated, unresolved, growing-up wound. In Alyson's case, she put down the guy's friends, especially his female friends, hoping that he would see her as being more special than they were. As you can imagine, it wasn't long before the guy decided he no longer wanted to hang out. Only Alyson couldn't understand why he started ignoring her text messages.

One day, Alyson ran into the guy at Starbucks and asked him what was up, why he'd stopped returning her messages. He felt put on the spot and stammered around before finally blurting out the truth: she pissed him off every time she dissed his friends. He said he'd known his friends longer than he'd known her, and he didn't appreciate her speaking negatively about them all the time. Not only that, because Alyson never had anything positive to say about his buddies or previous girlfriends, she made him feel like he was wrong for liking people she didn't like.

Alyson was stunned. She had no idea what kind of effect her constant dissing had had on this guy: he was willing to end their friendship *and* possible budding romance. She promised she would stop dissing and find other, more constructive ways of addressing those growing-up wounds that made her feel small. In a few months, she was making more friends and gaining people's trust and respect. She even got to hang out more with the guy she liked as he eventually began to warm up to her again. He started taking her friendship seriously and was thankful she had stopped putting down his friends.

Judging other people is a human trait that most of us need to work on. It's almost an instinct for girls to put down a guy's female friends or previous girlfriends out of insecurity or jealously. And if you're dating a guy who happens to have a lot of female friends, those friends can be intimidating. Of course his guy friends can cause you to feel a twang of insecurity when he wants to hang with them and not you. It's just as easy to diss his guy buddies, so be careful.

DR. JENN SAYS...

If you are dissing because you feel jealous, try being honest with a guy about how you feel instead of attacking his friends.

The next time you feel the urge to put down a guy's female friends, remember this: everyone has a past. We all have people we've come to know before a new friend or love interest comes into our lives—including him, including you.

So what if he's known a lot of girls before he met you? He didn't choose to be with any of them the way he wants to be with you. He didn't see any of them as his special Dream Girl, the way that he sees you; and even if he did, that doesn't matter because he doesn't see them that way anymore. After all, he's chosen *you*. If you like him as he much as he likes you, you'll realize these girls are all just friends, just pieces of his past. You'll see that they pose no threat to you whatsoever. If there's any threat at all, it's the one you pose to yourself when you give in to the urge to diss. If you put down his friends, he just might pick them *over you*.

Dream Girls know how challenging it can be to deal with all the emotions that arise when the guys they like also have female friends. But they also know that, when you work through any jealousy or mistrust, you get to a much better place within yourself and within your relationship.

We'll talk more about jealousy later in the chapter. In the meantime, let's see what guys have to say about dissing:

((((What Guys Are Saying About Girls Who Diss Their Friends

It's your opinion, honey, and I'm upset that you don't like them, but they're my friends, not yours.
     —Ben, England

Any girl that disses my friends has got to go. My friends were there before her and will be there once she's gone. If she doesn't like your friends, she doesn't really like you and will try to change you.
     —G. Z., USA

First, I make sure they [my friends] know that I know they're my friends. Then, I stand up for my mates. A girl should know all my friends are awesome people. If they weren't, then they wouldn't be my friends.
     —Mike, Australia

If she disses them when we are alone, then I would think that maybe she was jealous because she thinks that I would rather be with them than with her ... or I'll just ask her to be nice to them because they are my friends, and I care for them. [But] if she disses them in public, I'll try to calm her down and maybe walk out of the area, and ask "What's wrong?"
—Karim, USA

A NAG IS AN OLD HORSE. IS THAT HOW YOU SEE YOURSELF?

Nagging is another form of badgering that guys feel strongly about. Guys view girls who nag as "bitches"—ouch! Now I realize it's hard to talk about nagging, let alone the reasons why girls (and guys) shouldn't do it, and not sound like a nag myself. It's impossible to discuss this topic without a lot of do's and don'ts. But there is so much about this topic that guys want you to know—especially when it comes to the things we do that can make us seem like a nag without meaning to—that I cannot emphasize enough how important it is for you to read it all.

Of course, it's easy for a girl to blame any nagging behavior she may exhibit on her hormones and think that makes everything A-OK. But it doesn't work that way.

what guys want you to know:

Guys want you to take responsibility for your nagging and stop making excuses for it.

Secret No. 25

Natalie, a nineteen-year-old college sophomore, used to fly off the handle once in a while and nag her boyfriend about the smallest things. She would demand he call her more often and tell him he couldn't wear clothes that she didn't like. She'd even bug him about his study habits and how late he stayed up. She had no clue how often she went into control-freak mode until her boyfriend said how tired he was of feeling picked on. She offered the excuse that she was just PMS-ing, but he didn't buy it. Not long after that, he walked.

That was a steep price to pay, but at least Natalie got the message. Now that she is more aware of how her unattractive behavior can push guys away, she doesn't nag as much.

In Natalie's defense, girls don't wake up in the morning and say, "Hey! I'm going to drive a guy crazy today with my nagging." It just happens. And yes, sometimes your hormones *are* off the charts and make you more prone to being a bit of a nag. I mean, who hasn't had a bad case of PMS? Just be careful not to let your hormones get the upper hand so that you turn into a nag and turn off any respect a guy may have for you.

PMS aside, maybe you have troubles at home. Maybe your parents are experiencing marital woes, and you lay in bed at night worrying about them. Or maybe your sister keeps borrowing your favorite pair of jeans without asking or your little brother is hanging out with a rough crowd. When things aren't going smoothly at home, you may find yourself taking out your frustration on others by nagging them, whether you mean to or not.

WHAT DO I NEED?

Nancy was a classic case of someone who nagged because her needs were not being met. Nancy felt that her friends were ignoring her, not returning text messages as soon as they used to, and excluding her from activities she used to be invited to. She couldn't understand what was happening; she hadn't argued with anyone; nor could she remember hurting anyone or treating anyone badly. And yet she felt increasingly alone. Even worse, she had no idea how to reach out and ask what was going on within her circle of friends. She just saw them slowly pulling away, one by one, for no apparent reason.

You know what happened next, right? Nancy began nagging her friends: she told them what she thought they should be doing because she thought *they* were the ones who got everyone else to ignore her. If that weren't enough, Nancy also started nagging guys she liked. It was all part of an unskilled attempt to fulfill her basic need, which was to get her friends to like her again and include her.

Nagging can come from a place of fear within us, as well as an attempt to control others. In Nancy's case, the more afraid and lonely she became, the more control she wanted over her friends. The more she wanted to control her friends, the more she nagged them. The more she nagged, the further she pushed her friends away, which only made her nag them more to make up for her fear and loneliness. This is what's known as a *vicious cycle*. You nag because you don't get what you need; when your needs slip even further away from you, you nag some more.

DR. JENN SAYS...

Nagging is a vicious cycle. I stopped creating my cycle by learning what I needed. You can, too.

That was what was happening with Nancy. The cycle escalated until she was really depressed.

What could Nancy have done differently? For one, she could have communicated her needs clearly instead of nagging. Nancy would have been better off had she simply taken notice of what was happening with her friends. They were beginning to ignore her. The next step would be for her to understand her feelings about the situation. Nancy was lonely, and she was worried that there was something wrong with her and it was her fault her friends were ignoring her.

Next, Nancy could have figured out what she needed. Did she need her friends to go back to their old behavior, or did she need more from them now? Or did she need or want something entirely different? Only Nancy could know for sure.

Finally, Nancy would have been better off to tell her friends what she needed and hoped for in the future. It's hard to stand up for ourselves and speak the truth, but clear communication helps us get what we need. It not only teaches others how we want to be treated, it can stop us from nagging and pushing people away.

What do you need to do in order to get your needs met from others? What do you need to do in order to get your needs met from the guy you like? Write your answers in the space on the following page.

What do you need to do in order to get your needs met by others? What do you need to do in order to get your needs met by the guy you like?

The better you understand your own needs, the less prone you'll be to resorting to nagging as a last-ditch effort to get what's lacking in your life.

One way to stop nagging, and to start showing love to yourself and others, is to simply pay attention to those moments when you feel the urge to nag. Instead of opening up your mouth and going into nag mode, keep your mouth shut and open your heart—to others, of course, but also to yourself.

Ask yourself, "What am I feeling that makes me want to nag? Am I scared, lonely, upset, or angry? Do I feel that I'm right and the guy I like is wrong and want to make sure he knows it?" Figure out what you're feeling and come up with at least one healthy way to deal with it.

Sometimes you'll figure out your feelings right on the spot and be able to stop nagging immediately. Other times, you won't. That's okay; this is important, so don't be afraid to take a break from a conversation if you need to. Tell the guy you're with that you need a moment. He may not understand right away, but he'll certainly appreciate it later that you took care of yourself and didn't nag him.

> **DR. JENN SAYS...**
>
> *Nagging is a sign that something is going on inside us that we're not comfortable with.*

You remember the point we made in Chapter Two about listening? Listening effectively is not about you but about showing respect to the guy you're with. Well, with nagging it's the other way around.

Nagging has nothing with do with the guy we're with. Instead it's all about us and what we're feeling. Not only that, nagging usually tells us *there's something wrong inside*, something within ourselves that we don't like or we just aren't comfortable with. The trick, of course, is *being aware* of what that something is and then *doing something about it.*

Here's a quick story about another Dream Girl rookie that illustrates our point. Let's call her Gwen. Gwen badly wanted to be a Dream Girl. She really did. She listened really well, she showed love by not gossiping, and she built herself a huge trust account with her guy.

Only problem was, Gwen nagged—a lot. Mostly it was about her guy's school work, and how she felt he didn't push himself hard enough.

Her nagging went on every week, and it got to the point where Gwen's guy dreaded the you-should-be-studying-harder talk. He felt that Gwen believed he would never amount to anything and became defensive whenever she started in.

You know where this is going. Before long, the nagging turned into full-blown fights.

When I spoke with Gwen, I asked her to identify the feeling or need beneath her nagging. At first she had no idea. But after she thought about it, she said she was worried her guy would be a slacker all his life. She was used to high standards for herself and wanted her guy to be just like her.

Once Gwen recognized the feeling behind her nagging, she was able to stop and be more supportive of her guy. She realized his learning disability was a problem for him and that he too, was afraid he wouldn't get too far if he didn't learn more. Having Gwen's support instead of her nagging gave him the courage to study a bit harder. And talking about his fears about his learning disability brought them a lot closer.

Now *that's* love in action.

Look at your needs, wants, and fears, and figure out how they play a role in your own nagging. Then work on whatever issues you need to work on to stop nagging and start loving.

I know you can do it ... and guys do, too.

What Guys Are Saying About Nagging

Girls who nag, nag, nag, make me crazy. I can't stand to be around them. They think they know everything and have to make sure you do everything right. It's annoying.
—Louis, USA

I dated a nag once. There was no way to make her happy, so I broke up with her. I realized the nagging was part of a problem deeper than just things in our relationship.
—Will, USA

I stay clear of girls who are going to be on my case all the time. How can you enjoy being with a girl like that when she can't relax and just go with the flow? It's crazy how many girls want to control your every move and bug you about everything they think is wrong with you. That's not what love is all about.
—Jay, USA

DO YOU REALLY WANT TO BE HIS MOTHER?

Guys want you to be their friends or girlfriends. They want you to be supportive, nurturing, and a good listener. They want to know that you are there for them. What they don't want, however, is for you to be their mother.

Now I realize that in your desire to be there a guy, it can be hard to resist the urge to hover over him like a momma bird in the nest. There's a fine line between showing your desire to be supportive and take care of him and making him feel like a helpless, little boy. You may mean well, but what you may not realize is that your tendency to mother him can make you seem to be far less of the Dream Girl than you actually are.

Let me share with you a story about a very nice girl named Annie. Annie liked to micromanage everything, including the lives of her friends. She was always giving them unwanted advice and putting on her mommy apron, metaphorically speaking. Before long she was doing the same thing to the guys she dated or liked: tying them to her apron strings, keeping them on a close leash, making sure they were okay, and fretting over every boo-boo they got. Of course, it not only got tiring, but one of her guy friends finally yelled at her and told her to knock it off: he didn't need *two* mothers.

Annie was embarrassed; she had no idea she was mothering so much. Now she is more aware of her mother-mode tendencies and stops before she goes overboard. Her friends enjoy hanging out with her again, while guys find her more attractive.

You'll see amazing growth in your friendships when stop handing out unwanted advice. Stop telling them what they should think and how they should act or feel., And stop trying to put a Band-Aid on every little scrape they get, whether they need one or not.

Think of a time when you just wanted someone to hear you out—only they jumped in and told you how to run your life instead. If you're like most people, you probably resented the intrusion. Even well-intentioned advice, when given without permission, can make the recipient feel small and inadequate. It's as if you're saying, "You can't be trusted to make good decisions about your life, so I have to do that for you."

That's what it feels like to guys when you mother them. You make them feel as if they can't do anything right. Who wants to be around anyone who makes you feel like that?

Bonus Secret

Guys don't want you to be their mom. They already love the one they have.

Your mothering instincts will be put to good use if and when you decide to have children. That precious ability will be valued more than you know by your little ones. Until then, you can still nurture, support, care, and show respect to guys without unwanted hovering and mothering. Letting guys figure out their own lives for themselves and decide on their own what they need to do is another way to show love in action. Not only will they appreciate that, it lets them know you trust them to find their way in this crazy world.

By the way, it goes without saying that the key word is *unwanted*. Obviously, if a guy asks for your help or advice, don't hesitate to step in. That's what Dream Girls do.

HOW TO UNTIE YOUR APRON STRINGS

What are some of the things girls do that guys consider unwanted mothering? Here's a short list:

- Checking up on him often to make sure he is "okay"
- Making sure he got home "okay" every night
- Reminding him of something he needs to do
- Reminding him to remember people's birthdays, etc.
- Asking him if he is sure he had enough to eat when he is done with his meal
- Fixing his hair if it's out of place

- Calling him to make sure he got up on time for school or work
- Picking out his clothes for him

Think about your own relationships. Be honest. Have you ever done anything to mother a guy? If the answer is yes, then write it below:

What have I done to mother a guy?

Now, what can you do to untie your apron and kick your mothering habit? The same thing you did to rid yourself of your desire to gossip and nag. Do some detective self-listening. Ask yourself what it is inside you that fuels your need to mother. For example, some girls find they need to mother either because they never bonded with their own mom or weren't nurtured enough as a child. So they attempt to heal that growing up wound by caring for others instead, hoping that they will get cared for in return. The problem, as always, is that it's amazingly easy to start putting others' needs before your own.

Your needs are just as important as anyone else's needs. As a matter of fact, no matter how well meaning you are, there will come a point where you won't do anyone any good unless you also take care of yourself. In fact, you need to take care of yourself *before* you care for others. Remember the preflight oxygen mask lesson from Chapter One? Knowing you should take care of yourself first can help keep you from mothering a guy. So what if your guy makes a mistake and forgets something or is late to school? Dream Girls know we learn best from our own mistakes; and they know that it's okay for him to make some.

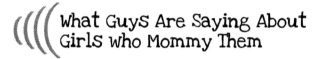

What Guys Are Saying About Girls Who Mommy Them

Don't mother me! I have a mom. I don't need you telling me what I need to be doing as well.
　　—Kyle, USA

I want a girlfriend, not a mother. How unsexy is that, to be with someone who smothers you all the time.
　　—Jessie, USA

At first I thought her attention was so cute. I mean, she seemed like she really cared about me. But after awhile, it pissed me off. I had to check in with her all the time, let her know I was okay, and she always told me how I should be living my life. Shit. She was like my mom!
　　—Allen, USA

JEALOUSY'S GRIP

As the saying goes, hell has no fury like a woman scorned. Jealousy is not a jewel in the Dream Girl crown; nor does it help you show love to others. But it's hard to not feel jealous and go berserk when your guy flirts overtly with other girls or leaves sexy comments on some hot babe's MySpace page. When we feel jealous, our limbic system—the part of our brain we learned about before—jumps into action by hijacking our ability to think rationally and logically. When that happens, of course, it's not a pretty sight.

"Hold up Dr. Jenn. You have mentioned the limbic system a few times now. What really goes on in our bodies when it is activated?"

Good question. Pretend you are in a car, either driving or riding shotgun. An oncoming car suddenly swerves into your lane coming at you head-on. Your brain will release a batch of chemicals (norepinephrine and adrenocorticotropic hormones to be exact), which will cause your bronchial tubes in your lungs to expand, your pupils to dilate, and your blood pressure and heart rate to increase; blood will be routed to your internal organs and muscles so you can quickly avoid a crash. After the car you are in swerves to safety, you will feel shaky and a bit disoriented. This is not the best time to be making rational decisions, is it? You are in survival mode, and logic goes out the window.

Since jealousy strikes us at our most vulnerable place, shattering our confidence to pieces, it can make us flip out, lash out, go ballistic, and do all sorts of awful things we later come to regret because we weren't thinking logically. Jealousy feels horrible in your body, heart, and mind and can make you act like a just-in-his-jeans girl. It can make you nag, gossip, leave nasty comments on people's profiles, send in-your-face text messages—you know, the kind of things that don't show respect to yourself or to others. No wonder jealous girls scare the heebie-jeebies out of guys, especially guys who know what it's like to feel a girl's wrath.

THE CONSEQUENCES OF JEALOUSY

Jealousy is hardly gender specific. Guys can be jealous, too, and they don't like how it feels any more than we do.

With that in mind, let's take a look at jealousy up close.

Fergie loved a guy named Donny. She thought the sun and moon rose in Donny's eyes. He was her prince charming. Fergie was thrilled that he loved her, too, but deep inside she worried that maybe he would find someone better than her. He was sooo perfect, she wondered if she really deserved him. Then, one day, Donny sent a sexy comment to a girl on MySpace. Fergie saw it and was so jealous that she tore up every picture of Donny she had. She burned all of his love letters and slashed to pieces the big stuffed baboon he had won for her at the fair. She texted him that it was over between the two of them.

No one was allowed to mention Donny's name in front of her. But the problem was Fergie still loved Donny even if no one was saying his name.

Months went by. Fergie was still jealous. She wrote really nasty comments on Donny's MySpace page where everyone could read what a jerk she thought he was. Donny didn't appreciate Fergie's actions, to say the least. Fergie even wrote a nasty note on Donny's car in bright red lipstick late one night.

The next morning, Fergie looked in the mirror and thought to herself, "I am losing it. This is crazy." She knew she was terrified she would lose Donny's love to the girl he had flirted with. Heck, she was afraid she would lose him to almost any girl, to be truthful. But she had dumped him for flirting, so she had lost him anyway.

Fergie worked on being more self-confident. She texted Donny and asked to talk to him. They had dinner together, and she explained to him how much her jealousy hurt and how she wanted to get over it. She also wanted to work on a relationship with him again. Donnie apologized for his comment to the other girl and explained how he was feeling a bit unappreciated by Fergie when he wrote it. He was just looking for someone to give him some positive feedback, nothing more. He said he was sorry for hurting Fergie.

Fergie and Donny both did a great job of listening to each other. They decided to give it another try and got back together. Fergie worked on her insecurities when they arose, and Donny did a better job of telling Fergie when he needed more attention from her. Fergie went one step further. Fergie forgave Donny for flirting with the other girl, and Donny forgave Fergie for her comments and the lipstick raid on his ride.

Now what if the story was different? What if Donny had cheated on Fergie before, and she knew about it? Her jealousy would have been aroused by her past experience with him. Old trust issues can be a hair trigger for jealousy, just as our own insecurities can be.

Jealousy is about our fear that the person we love will give someone else the affection we believe belongs to us. No matter the cause of our jealousy, it makes us create an enemy image of someone. Notice how Donny became a label to Fergie. He was a jerk. That's an enemy image. That's seeing others as things, not as human beings who can make mistakes, screw up, hurt us, and feel bad about hurting us. And when we see others as things, instead of human, you can bet we can do some real damage to them and to ourselves in our state of jealousy.

If you feel jealous often, it's a good idea go back to the growing-up wounds quiz in Chapter One and take it again. Ask yourself the following questions:

What might have happened in the past that causes me to feel insecure and threatened so often?

How can I get past my old growing-up pains?

Being aware of your jealousy is the first step in learning how to tame its monstrous grip on your life. Gaining more confidence is a good cure for jealousy. When you feel good about yourself and your ability to create healthy relationships, you are less apt to feel squeezed by jealousy's grasp. Ironing out your trust issues is another way to help get out of jealousy's grip. Talking about your concerns about being able to trust your guy means you will need to be a detective listener and not put him on the defensive, or you may never resolve the issues.

GUYS FEEL JEALOUSY TOO

If your guy is feeling jealous, ask him what's causing it. Maybe you've accidentally triggered an old growing-up wound that he still has to stop and deal with. Use your best detective listening skills and ask what's true for him. Don't defend, don't attack, just listen and help him sort things out. If you are doing something on purpose to make him feel jealous, better think twice about that plan of action.

Guys don't like having their hearts played. Making a guy jealous isn't the way to keep his interest or keep him. It's just a way to make him feel lousy and resent you for those feelings. Making a guy feel jealous isn't respectful, as our friend Patty learned the hard way.

Patty had a crush on a guy she met her first semester in high school. She only had one class with him, and she wished she could run into him more often. She didn't know his friends, so she didn't know how to get closer to him. She was excited when she saw him at a party at a friend's house. She made small talk with him but couldn't figure out if he was interested or not. When some of her guy friends came into the room, she started flirting with them, hoping that it would make her crush feel as if she was sought after and a "catch." She hoped he would be the tiniest bit jealous and want her to flirt and talk with him all night.

He wasn't impressed with her flirting and ignored her the rest of the night. He just wasn't into the game playing. He knew that if Patty was willing to start off a relationship using jealousy as a manipulation ploy, she would probably be willing to use it once she was in a solid relationship. He didn't want to be with a girl who had to resort to trying to make him jealous to get his attention.

DR. JENN SAYS...

Don't play the jealousy game.

Had Patty used some detective listening skills, she could have avoided trying to make him feel jealous. She would have made him feel respected and cared for had she just *listened* to him; instead, she was disrespectful and treated him in a way she would not have wanted to be treated. She didn't put herself in his shoes at all.

Another girl named Jody played a similar jealousy game, but she used the Internet to make her guy jealous. She left sexy comments on her friend's MySpace profiles. She knew her guy lurked around, checking up on her, only she kinda liked that. She got off whenever he went off on her about her silly game playing. To Jody, the more her guy ranted and raved, the more she thought it meant he truly loved her. After all, if he was jealous it meant he loved her, right?

Jody didn't think about how much she was wounding her guy with her jealousy game. That's certainly not love in action.

Love takes into consideration what others may feel due to our actions. Love makes people feel supported and cared for. But Jody made her guy feel insecure and not cared for. Jody cared more for her own ego than she did about her guy's heart. Needless to say, he didn't stick around for too long. He didn't know how to listen like a good detective; and for that matter, neither did Jody. With neither one of them knowing how to figure out what made her want to make him jealous, they didn't stand much of a chance.

Playing the jealousy game is no match for listening like a good detective. Guys crave true attention. When you give them your focus and your open ears and hearts, you capture their focus and their hearts. Making a guy jealous doesn't prove he loves you or is going to stay with you.

Dream Girls know not to play the jealousy game. They know that love in action means wanting the best for someone else, not jerking that person's heart around.

what guys want you to know:

*Guys don't like girls
who get jealous too easily.*

Secret No. 26

Bonus Secret

*Guys don't like girls
who try to make them jealous.*

What Guys Are Saying About Jealous Girls and Game Players

Girls who flirt with other guys in front of me make me lose my trust in them. If they are able to flirt in front of me, what are they doing when I am not around? If the girl is trying to make me jealous and like her more, it doesn't work. I don't want to be with someone like that.

—Curtis, USA

My last girlfriend was jealous of everything. Every time my phone rang, she had to know who is was and what they wanted. I couldn't take her insecurity.

—James, USA

My girlfriend never tries to make me jealous. She always asks how I am feeling about our relationship and how I feel about her friends and what she is up to. She goes out of her way to make sure I feel secure. I appreciate that. It makes me feel like she really cares about me.

—John, USA

I wish girls understood that guys have friends who are girls, and we don't want to give them up just because the girl we like is jealous. My last girlfriend made me choose [between] her or my female friend I had known all my life. I didn't know if my girlfriend and I would last, but I knew my female friend and I would always be friends, so I dumped the new girlfriend.

—Kyle, USA

Girls need to know that guys have girlfriends, and we aren't cheating on our girlfriends with them. They are just friends! Nothing more.

—Jesse, USA

The best [scenario] is when my girlfriend likes my female friends, and we can all hang out and get along. It reduces so much drama.
—John, USA

Now that we've looked at all the things that show us what love doesn't look like, here's a quick quiz.

❑ Do I gossip about people I don't like?
❑ Do I leave nasty comments on MySpace when I'm jealous?
❑ Do I play the jealousy game to mess with a guy's heart?
❑ Do I hover over guys and mother them when they don't want me to?
❑ Do I diss my guy's friends? Do I diss myself?
❑ Do I nag at my guy a lot?

If you answered yes to any of these questions, take a look at what you are feeling. Are you scared? Angry? Do you feel disrespected? Are you nagged at home? Find out what's true for you, and see if you can heal whatever drives you to gossip, nag, diss, mother, or play the jealousy game. Can you take care of your needs first, so that you ultimately have more to give to a relationship? If you need help with finding out what's true for you, turn back to Chapter Three and write down more thoughts. See what new things you come up with.

Dream Girls know that love is an action. It is not always a feeling. You can dislike people and still show them love. Human beings aren't perfect. Dream Girls accept this fact and deal with it by showing compassion, empathy, and care to everyone they meet, because that's what love *really* looks like.

So what do you do when you feel yourself in the clutches of jealousy? First, just breathe. Really, *just breathe.* When you find yourself at the end of your rope, don't grab your cell phone and start texting. Slow down and do ten deep, calming breaths instead. Then think about the person you who made you jealous. Instead of fixating on how badly that person wounded you, think about how wounded he or she is and how human his or her mistake is. Then ask yourself if you can stop the drama inside your brain and forget about how much of an asshole you think that person is—and simply forgive him or her instead.

If you can do that, if you can resist the pull of jealousy and bring yourself to forgive, believe me, you're well on your way to becoming a Dream Girl. I am not saying it's easy, but it's worth the effort.

Here are the differences between a Dream Girl and a just-in-his-jeans-girl when it comes to love in action. Which column do you fall more into?

DREAM GIRLS	JUST-IN-HIS-JEANS GIRLS
• Ask for what they need	• Nag others to try to get them to do what they want
• Respectfully confront someone who has upset them or dissed them	• Spread gossip about the person who has dissed or upset them
• Let guys make their own decisions	• Smother guys with mothering
• Know that making a guy feel heard and understood is the key to building a healthy relationship	• Manipulate guys with nagging, gossiping, and jealousy in order to try to build a relationship
• Know that comments on MySpace can have a big impact and, therefore, do not leave any messages that could hurt others	• Lash out and leave nasty comments on MySpace so others know they are mad at the person they are flaming
• Listen to what makes a guy jealous	• Think it's cute that they can make a guy jealous
• Take care of their needs first	• Do not take care of their needs

• Keep their mouths shut whenever they have a negative judgment about others	• Diss people with little regard for whoever hears them

Love isn't nagging, mothering, dissing or playing the jealousy game. Those things only tarnish the sparkle of your Dream Girl crown. Learning to avoid the things that are not loving and to focus on showing respect for yourself and your guy will make you shine in the most attractive light.

One of the big mistakes Dream Girl trainees make is that they sell themselves short. When you discount yourself, guys will, too. The next chapter reveals the secrets guys wish you knew about discount behaviors.

Don't Sell Yourself Short

"There was this girl who wore tank tops, booty shorts, and she talked shit about other girls a lot. She liked having all the attention. She had to drink herself to sleep some nights and partied a lot. Even though she had problems, I liked her, and I really wanted to help her feel better about herself. She told me she liked me, too, but then I found out she was hooking up with my older brother's friends. Every day, it was some new drama that she wanted me to focus on about her. I finally told her I couldn't deal with it anymore. She needed to find her own self-confidence and figure out her problems. I couldn't help her."

—Name withheld by request, USA

"I like a girl who leaves a little bit to the imagination. I don't want to see every part of her body. If her thong is hanging out, she loses my respect. There is something special about a girl not everyone gets to see. First off, it's trashy if she shows too much of herself and, second, what's left for me? If she discounts herself, she counts me out."

—Neil, Canada

The dollar store may be a cool place to shop for great savings, but discounts in a relationship don't save you anything. In fact, they can cost you big time.

Self-confidence and self-respect go hand in hand. One leads to the other. So it shouldn't surprise you to know that many of the things that prevent you from attaining respect—like your growing-up wounds, your Itty Bitty Shitty Committee, or all those fashion and beauty ads that show what a "perfect, sexy, beautiful" girl is *supposed* to look like—can also screw up your confidence.

Confidence is like trust, in that it's super fragile. It takes a long time to build, a short time to destroy, and a long time to build back up again. And just as a lack of trust can make you feel empty, so can a lack of confidence. When your confidence ain't there, *it just ain't there*, and there's nothing you can do to fake it.

That's because true confidence comes from within. And that's the key. The only thing you really need to be confident is simply to be yourself.

what guys want you to know:

Guys are drawn to the inner beauty that self-confidence provides.

Secret No. 27

Obviously, that's easier said than done. Girls today face too many obstacles that can trip up their confidence—or, make them seem less confident than they could be. Some of these obstacles, like wearing clothes that are too revealing, are behaviors triggered in response to fashion ads we see plastered all over the media. Girls dress like the models they see in the music videos or in Abercrombie and Fitch catalogs because they think that's what guys want. Other behaviors, like partying too much (be it drinking, drugging, or both), can be brought on by peer pressure or the need to be accepted. Then there's acting like a drama queen or a spotlight girl, which, besides being rude, obnoxious, and disrespectful, are behaviors that often cover up a lack of confidence in oneself.

Guys call these behaviors "discount behaviors" because they can literally sell a girl short.

CONFIDENCE IS FOCUSING ON WHAT YOU HAVE

So how do you build strong self-confidence instead of falling back on discount behaviors? Don't focus on what you don't have. Focus on what you *do* have. Think about it. We each have at least one area of our lives that we feel confident about. Everyone has at least one skill or ability he or she really excels in. Ask yourself right now, what are the things that I know I do well? It can be anything: singing, driving, typing, reading, acting, cooking, baking, doing math, playing sports, writing, drawing, designing, enjoying the outdoors ... whatever it happens to be. That's the fun thing about taking inventory of ourselves. There's no right or wrong answer. Think of all the things that you do well and write them down:

Memo to Me:
Things that I do well

Now that you've made your list, think about how you felt when you wrote those things down. What sensations did you feel in your body when you thought about the things you're good at? Did you feel calm? Tingly? Excited? Exuberant?

Memo to Me:
When I think about the things that I do well, it makes me feel...

What words would you use to describe how you felt? Write those down as well.

Now that you've made your list of how it feels when you feel confident, go back to the list you made in Chapter One—you know, the one where you wrote down how your body feels whenever you feel respect. Compare the two lists. Okay, how many words on your "When I Think About The Things I Do Well" list were also on your "When I Feel Respect" list? I bet there were a few.

Let's say tomorrow is the day you take your college-entry exam. You've taken the pre-exam course after school, so you have a good idea of what to expect. And yet you're still a nervous wreck. Your chances of going to the school you want to go to are riding on how well you do tomorrow, and that's just freaking you out.

It's okay to feel a little nervous. After all, you're about to do something you've never done before. You wouldn't be human if you didn't feel nervous or less than completely confident. The trick, of course, is to keep your level of nervousness under control so that it doesn't affect your ability to perform as well as you know you can.

So if you're nervous about taking the college-entry exam, forget about the "college entry" part and focus on the "exam" instead. An exam is just another word for test, right? You've taken lots of tests before; not only that, taking tests is something you happen to do very well. You know how to study for a test. You know how to pace yourself during the one hour or two hours you have to take the test, so that you answer every question in each section of the test as best you can. And most important of all, you know that your preparation and pacing always pays off.

Now how do you feel? A lot more relaxed, I'll bet.

That's what happens when you focus on what you have—or in this case, what you know—instead of what you don't have. By looking at the college-entry exam as just another test, you've turned an unknown situation into something you know. By turning it into something you know, something you have done well before, you remind yourself of what confidence feels like in your body. That feeling of confidence will carry you through.

> **DR. JENN SAYS...**
>
> *If you've done something successful once before, you know you can do it again.*

Granted, reminding yourself of how good confidence feels is not an instant cure. That's because self-confidence, like self-respect, detective listening, trust, showing love in action, and all the other characteristics of being a Dream Girl, takes time to develop and a lifetime to maintain. You have to keep reminding yourself over and over until you feel good again, strong again, kind of like how you have to recharge your cell phone or iPod. You have to keep recharging you!

NEVER BE AFRAID TO LEARN

The more you focus on what you have or what you know, the easier it will be to recall that confident feeling whenever you need it. And that's something I can tell you with absolute confidence. However, one of the worst things you can do is to avoid doing things you don't feel confident doing. Why? Because you'll never stretch yourself beyond your limited comfort zone and grow to do bigger and better things. Remember, everything you know how to do in your life, you had to learn at some point.

You came into this world a helpless infant. Had there not been someone to feed you, bathe you, change your diapers, and help you learn things, you never would have survived.

So how do you get over your fear of learning? The same way you managed to take that college-entry exam. You break things down into manageable pieces. You take things in small steps. No one climbs Mount Everest in a day. They take their time. They get used to higher altitude, let their bodies adjust, and then they press on. That's the way to learn anything that seems insurmountable. *Move forward, rest, get used to your new skills, then press on again.* There's no hurry. Before you know it, you'll have the confidence you need to take yourself to the next level. That's what Dream Girls do!

what guys want you to know:

Being confident does not mean being perfect. Guys want you to know that your best is always good enough, so long as you continue to try.

Secret No. 28

Of course, lack of confidence can stem from things other than feeling you lack skills or ability. We can lack confidence about our appearance, our IQ, our social skills, or just about anything. Everyone, at one time or another, worries about one thing or another. But no matter what you're worried about or what causes you fear or doubt, the steps you take to restore your confidence remain the same: *focus on what you do have* and highlight that instead of worrying about what you believe you lack.

Say you have curly, red hair that you absolutely hate. Before you think about changing the color of your hair (or perhaps hacking it off altogether), take a good long look at your pretty green eyes. Notice how much they sparkle in contrast to your flaming red mane. Play up that feature, and you'll never worry about your hair again.

Whatever area you lack confidence in, look for a small part of that area that you do well in, and believe that even that small area will continue to grow so long as you continue to nurture it.

Remember the exercise in Chapter One about the invitation? Invite guys to see the best in you, whether it's seeing your best physical attributes or your best character traits. You don't have to become a drama queen or a spotlight girl to get a guy to see your best. It will shine all by itself!

You are a unique, fabulous person. And you will be better at being yourself than trying to be someone you aren't.

Learning to accept who you are is challenging. It's easy to pay lip service to saying you like yourself and that you feel confident. But we all have areas we want to make better. It's important to accept yourself, and equally important to work at being your best. Take the time to work on what you want to change. Do

DR JENN SAYS...

It's okay to be you.

so with compassion and caring. Treat yourself as if you are your own best friend. Don't whine about what you don't like about yourself. That's really unattractive. Don't make excuses as to why you can't change; at least make an effort. Guys will know you are doing your best to be your best, that's what's really appealing and attractive.

What Guys Are Saying About Confidence

It's all about confidence. Too many girls think "I'm not good enough," and it simply isn't true. I look for confidence. It's a huge turn-on.
—Zac, USA

I have learned that all girls either sell themselves short or are overconfident [about] themselves. I have learned in the past six months that those types of girls are not what I want. I

like girls who are strong-willed and who can think and act on their feet. No offense to women in general, but I cannot stand stupid girls—ones who think it's cool to act like children and still party when they are supposed to be responsible adults. Girls nowadays need to learn not to try to be like everyone else. They need to start thinking on their own, be their own person. Guys like intelligent women: ones who can rival them in actual conversations, females who are not afraid to speak their mind and tell it how it is. Women belittle themselves so much, and a lot of guys think it's wrong. Be who you want to be, not what others expect.
      —Art, USA

Women need to realize that they control the universe. Society seems to be male-dominated, but women are the ones with the real power!
      —Mike, USA

If you're smart ... flaunt it. Don't use it to the point of being conceited and snobbish—guys hate overconfidence as much as girls hate it in guys—but don't be afraid to show your intelligence. Show it for the sake of you and not the sake of impressing. Know who you are, and know what you want, and know what you're willing to do to get it.
      —Justin, USA

Just do your best. Guys don't expect perfection all the time. If you make a mistake, laugh about it. Who cares? It's okay. When you don't put so much pressure on yourself to be perfect, we know you won't drive us crazy to be perfect, either. No one is perfect.
      —Will, USA

PULL UP AND BUTTON UP
(A QUICK PRIMER ON HOW DREAM GIRLS DRESS)

Now you would think that young men today would drool over the chance to catch a free peek at your goodies. I mean, that's the image we see in practically every teen movie, music video, or advertisement made today, right? When a girl isn't parading around in a plunging tank top and micro miniskirt, she's bending over suggestively so that her thong or G-string rides up over the back of her pants, flashing her butt crack plain as day. Ooooh ... sexy. That's what guys want to see, right?

Wrong. That may be the case with guys in the movies, but it isn't what guys want if they want you to be their girlfriend.

Girls, the "whale tail" is not an attractive look, no matter what your body shape. Guys today just aren't into that. Don't believe me? Okay, then, let's flip it around. Do you want to see a guy's butt crack when he bends over? Ewww, of course not—that's gross. Guys I interviewed said they didn't like seeing whale tails, and wish girls would pull their pants up.

Or taking it to another extreme, consider Britney's now infamous beaver shot that was seen 'round the world few years ago. You might think most guys got off on the thought of her going commando, but it turns out the opposite is true. Most guys thought she just sold herself short by exposing herself. Lesson learned: If you're seated wearing a dress, make sure you (1) cross your legs or keep them together and (2) wear something underneath. That goes for whether you're within range of a camera/cell phone/video cam or not.

Believe it or not, women once wore high-neck dresses that ran all the way down to the floor. That was the fashion. They wore long sleeves and buttoned-up collars and gloves and stockings and layered petticoats and boots laced up to the ankle. The simple turn of an ankle from under a woman's skirt was enough to drive a man crazy. Why? Because everything was covered, nothing was revealed. So on those rare occasions when a man caught the slightest peek of a woman's neckline or bare shoulder, it was really, really sexy, simply because he was getting a chance to see the forbidden.

Of course, between flip skirts, booty shorts, tank tops, camisoles, sheer blouses, micro mini dresses, and other low-cut, high-hemmed fashions, guys today see so much flesh they're practically desensitized to it. That's really too bad, because a woman's body is so much more alluring when it's not shoved in a guy's face 24/7.

I'm not suggesting we throw out micro minis and go back to high-neck dresses; and for that matter, guys aren't suggesting that, either. What I am saying (and guys are, too) is that when it comes to the kind of girls they love the most, sometimes the old ways are better. There's no need to flash all your goodies when a quick peek can be just as effective (and sometimes, even more so!).

what guys want you to know:

Guys are tired of seeing so much skin.

Secret No. 29

Look, I'm no prude. And I'm not your mother. As far as I'm concerned, you can dress sexy whenever you want, if that's what you want to do. But before you do, before you squeeze yourself into that teeny-tiny tube dress and meet your friends at the mall, ask yourself if you're sending an "invitation" you may not mean to send. If you're looking to meet guys, how do you want them to see you? Like a sex object? Girls who dress like hoochie mommas or pole dancers certainly give off that vibe.

Okay, maybe you're not looking to hook up. Maybe you've just lost twenty pounds after weeks of working out at the gym. Maybe you simply want everyone to see just how great you look in that dress after all that hard work. There's nothing wrong with that. After all, you've got that feeling of confidence coursing through your body. You set a goal, you accomplished it, and now you feel good all over, so good, you want the rest of the world to know it.

But what if you meet a guy who you think is someone special? He may not think the same about you because you're wearing that teeny-tiny dress. Guys don't mind a little flash and tease, but only at the appropriate time, like when it's you and him, alone, together. That's when you make him feel special. But when you show up in a dress like that and show everything off in front of everyone else at the mall, what guy is going to feel like he's special to you?

That's what I mean about "selling yourself short." All the values you follow to become a Dream Girl get easily overlooked when you dress like a just-in-his-jeans girl.

Personal fashion style is personal. We each have our own sense of what our clothes say about us. Some girls dress Goth, some dress preppy, and others prefer hoodies and sweats. There is no right or wrong answer when it comes to your personal fashion style. Just keep in mind that our choice of clothes is an indication of our values, an open window for how we'd like others to see us. Be mindful of what you are inviting others to believe about you through your clothing.

DR. JENN SAYS...

Our clothes are an expression of who we are. Pay attention to what your clothes say about you.

(((What Guys Are Saying About Girls whose Clothes are too Revealing

There isn't a guy in the world who is gonna look at your thong as it hangs out of your pants or look at your chest that's busting out of your tight shirt, and say "Damn! Love at first sight. I want to marry her!"
—Robert, USA

Sexy isn't slutty or skanky. Sexy is elegant and confident.
—Walter, USA

When her clothes are too short or too small, I lose respect for her.
—Ike, Congo

Girls who are too scantily clad or wear see-through things or shirts that look like lingerie, lose my respect.
—Roberto, Mexico

Please tell girls to button it up. We are tired of seeing it all.
—Paul, USA

I wish girls knew that guys are going to pay attention to them even if they don't act or dress slutty and that self-respect will attract guys.
—Josh, USA

HOW HEARTY DO YOU PARTY?

Want the recipe for another discount behavior? Just add booze or drugs, and, bingo, there you are! Just how hearty you party can make the difference between guys seeing you as a Dream Girl or another just-in-his-jeans-girl. First, know that underage drinking and most party drugs are illegal. Not only that, using alcohol and or drugs harms your growth in a lot of ways. For every year you can put off experimenting with intoxicants the better off you'll be. And when you do turn 21, and can legally drink, doing so in moderation is always best.

Having said that, some of you are still going to party. If you choose to indulge, the key, as always, is to do so in moderation. Drinking and drugging too much is not only unattractive, it can be dangerous and life-threatening for girls and guys alike.

So what is too much? That often depends on the substance involved and the size, shape, and makeup of the individual. With alcohol, some people can feel wasted after one shot of tequila, while others can down a couple of drinks and not feel a thing. In other words, not all tolerance levels are created equal.

With drugs (and alcohol) there's addiction concerns. Rehabs and 12 Step programs are filled with girls and guys your age. While some drugs are more potent than others, the dangers of addiction are the same whether it's marijuana or cocaine you are hooked on. The best advice I can give you for a number of reasons is *just say NO to drugs*. It sounds so corny, but it's true.

Saying no can be hard, I know. Dr. Donald Dahl, a psychiatrist at the University of Pittsburg explains that teens' brains are wired for risk taking. The teenage years are a time in your lives when you want to assert your independence, or at least find out who you are and what works or doesn't work for you. In some ways, it's the most vulnerable time of your life; yet, at the same time, if you're like most teens, you never feel vulnerable at all. You don't think about the consequences of drinking or drugging, and you certainly don't think about the dangers of overdoing it. You don't think that you'll be the one to die from taking "E" or downing too many beers, yet teens die every year from alcohol poisoning, adverse reactions to drugs and overdoses. I didn't think about those things when I was your age, and probably your parents didn't either. After all, if you're like most teenagers you think you're going to live forever.

But just because your brain is more wired to take risks or enjoy certain sensations, that doesn't make it okay to fry your brain with legal or illegal substances. After all, just as the rest of your body continues to grow and change during your teenage years, so does your brain. As a matter of fact, your prefrontal cortex—the part of the brain where logical, rational decision making processes occur—doesn't stop growing until your mid twenties. This means that the drinking and drugging you do now *really does* affect the health of your brain in the future. Hopefully, you will take these words to heart by keeping your alcohol and drug experimentation very limited, if at all, and not become a huge partier.

Girls drink too much to overcome their low self-esteem or to feel more confident. Some party out of sheer boredom, while others self-medicate to calm nerves or overcome depression or anxiety. Peer pressure can make you feel like you have to play flip cups or do belly shots or fire up the bong or melt ice. Whatever your reasons are for choosing to consume, bear in mind that when you overdo it, not only can you make yourself sick, but you can also sell yourself short in the process.

Most guys know that a girl who is out of control on any substance is a girl with little self-respect. Not only that, when you party to the point where your judgment or reflexes are impaired, you put yourself in a position where you can be humiliated, harmed, and a whole lot worse.

That's why Dream Girls never party to the point where they leave themselves vulnerable.

what guys want you to know:

Guys want you to know that girls who are too into alcohol or drugs aren't what they are looking for in a romantic partner.

Secret No. 30

Oh, sure, there'll always be some guys who will party along with you no matter what because they think you're hilarious when you're bombed. But don't kid yourself into thinking they'll ever take you seriously as a romantic partner. Why should they, when every time they see you, you're downing shots, lying in your own vomit, or waking up with your clothes disheveled?

That's the lesson that a girl named Ali unfortunately learned the hard way.

Ali was a senior in high school and had a crush on a guy. She only talked to him a few times, but he seemed to like her, too. It turns out that Ali's friends all liked to party, so she figured, "Maybe I should start drinking, too."

One night, she went out to a friend's house whose parents were out of town and joined in a game of flip cups. The guy Ali liked was there, too. At some point, some other guy pulled out a bottle of vodka and encouraged the girls to let the guys do belly shots. It wasn't too long before belly shots turned into breast shots. Many of the girls, including Ali, took turns lying on the kitchen table as guys sucked vodka from in between their breasts.

What a nice image to project, especially in front of a guy you hope will like you.

Of course, the next thing she knew, Ali was in the bathroom, topless, puking her guts up. After staggering out of the bathroom, she picked up her shirt, put it back on, and slouched on the couch. She was dazed and still feeling her head spin when she noticed a guy sitting next to her. Ali beamed with joy; it was the guy she liked!

"Hey," she said. "What's happening?"

"I just called a cab," he said. "I think you need to get home."

"You're probably right," Ali said as she put her hand to her head. "Things got a little crazy." She paused a little before reaching for her purse. *Maybe he really likes me,* she thought. *Maybe I should give him my number.*

"Wanna do something tomorrow?" she asked.

"I don't think so, Ali."

Ali didn't understand. He'd just called a cab for her. That must mean he cares for her, right? "Don't you want to go out with me?"

"I thought you were different, Ali," he continued. "I didn't think you were the type of girl who'd let guys do breast shots on her."

At that moment, Ali realized that whatever attraction this guy may have had for her had been sucked away like the booze from her chest.

The moral of the story, of course, is that when a girl is under the influence, she will often do or say things that disrespect herself as well as others.

Alcohol and drugs remove your normal "governor." That's one reason why sex happens way too frequently when girls and guys party. Things have a way of going too far, whether we mean them to or not.

Think about it. You're sprawled on a table with your top off, and some drunken guy is licking booze off your chest. Your inhibitions are down, but remember, *so are his.* There's no chaperon in the house; nor is there anyone else in the room. What makes you think he won't also think about grabbing your chest, reaching up your skirt, or pulling down your pants while he unbuckles his?

When you have to ask, "*I did what* last night?" and you shudder when your friends fill in the details maybe it's time to assess your party-hearty ways.

"But, Dr. Jenn, what if I know exactly what I want, and I want to get drunk and have a guy screw me?"

Hey, it's your life. If you think you are in control of the situation, nothing I can say will stop you. Just don't get your panties in a bunch when you realize just how undignified you look in that video he took of you that night with his cell phone—you know, the one that's now all over YouTube, MySpace, Facebook, and every other uploadable video Web site for all the world to see. After all, you knew exactly what you were doing. And you're right, he certainly did screw you—and now the rest of the world knows it too. "Now you really sound like my mother, Dr. Jenn!" Well, mom's worry about their daughters, what can I say? I'm not saying that sex is wrong or bad, I just want you to think about how you go about having sex. Getting plastered to have sex doesn't sound like a lot of self-respect or self- confidence is in your life.

Remember, Dream Girls don't put themselves in a compromising position or let themselves be strong-armed to party. Nor do they strong-arm guys to party with them.

If you or someone you know parties too much and doesn't know when to stop, there are steps you can take to help yourself or them take control.

First and foremost, *talk to your parents* if you can. I know it's hard to believe, but they were once teenagers, too. Let them know what you've been up to. If you're afraid your partying is getting out of hand, ask them to help. If your parents can't help you or aren't willing to discuss this topic with you, is there another adult you can talk to? It could be an older sibling, an aunt or uncle, a neighbor, a teacher, a counselor, or anyone else you know and trust. Adults have been around the block a few times themselves; they know more about drinking and drugs than you might think.

Whoever you turn to, *be honest.* Honesty about your life is always the key to maintaining a level of control. And people can't help you if you don't give them all the information.

I hope you won't go out and party too much, but if you do, at least educate yourself on some safety issues. First, don't drink on an empty stomach. In 1994, a team of Swedish researchers discovered that safer

DR JENN SAYS...

Don't be afraid to reach out for help if you think you party too much.

consumption involves eating before you drink so that your stomach slows down the absorption of alcohol. Drinking a glass of water in between each glass of booze also helps. Be aware: taking over-the-counter pain meds before you go to bed in the hopes of warding off a hangover can lead to permanent or fatal liver damage. You should also know binge drinking can impair your ability to make good decisions even after your hangover has ended, and the impairment is worse for women. You may feel fine, but your brain doesn't.

"Pharm" parties are popular these days since so many prescription drugs are easily obtained. Know that mixing prescription drugs can be lethal very quickly. If you want to get high from a prescription drug, understand that just because it is legal for the person it was prescribed for, doesn't mean it's legal or safe for you to take it. And if you're getting high from your own meds, know that increasing doses, especially drugs for ADHD, can put your cardiovascular system into overdrive.

No matter what you do, make sure you have a designated driver. You need to arrange ahead of time for a licensed sober person to drive you home. If you ever find yourself in a situation where the person responsible for driving you is under the influence, find another ride. Dream Girls don't endanger themselves or others on the highway—ever. And for the record, underage drinking is illegal in every state, whether you drive or not. Having said that, Dream Girls know partying can be part of teenage explorations, but they know that participating in those explorations can lead to becoming a just-in-his-jeans girl, as fast as you can say "beer goggles." Be careful out there!

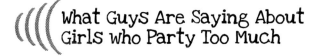

What Guys Are Saying About Girls who Party Too Much

Ladies, drinking too much isn't attractive!
—Steve, England

I can't stand to see a girl drunk off her ass at a party or a club. It's gross. I have never seen a drunk female who wasn't a total

mess. I would hate to date her even when she was sober, now that I know what she is really like when she is drunk.
—Adam, USA

If you drink for confidence, find another way to get it. Liquid courage is false courage. You usually end up doing something out of character and then have to apologize for it and only lose even more of your confidence. Moderation!
—Sasha, USA

DETHRONE YOUR DRAMA QUEEN

Let's face it: all of us love attention, especially when we accomplish something we know to be important. As we've said before, when we feel good about ourselves, when we reach a goal or know we've done the right thing, our confidence level goes up, and we want our friends and family to know how good we feel, so *they* can share in our happiness, too. Those are all times when it's perfectly cool to call attention to yourself.

It's just that, without a sense of moderation, spotlight seekers and drama queens not only annoy others but sell themselves short in the process. After all, if your spotlight is so bright that you can't see anyone else in front of you, then it's time to adjust the wattage.

Now it's time to shine the light on all you girls who want to be in the spotlight, including drama queens, queen bees, and girls who proudly wear T-shirts that say, *"It's all about me!"*

Why do so many girls love drama and attention? Probably because girls' brains are wired differently than guys' brains are. Girls are more verbal and deal with their emotions in a different way than guys do. Girls are more expressive about their emotions, and they talk more. To some guys, that alone can look like drama. But the real drama queens are the girls who constantly create drama for attention.

All of us have probably known at least one drama queen in our lives. You know the kind of girl I'm talking about. *Everything* is a problem to her. Everything is about her issues—her looks, her weight, her job, her grades, her boyfriend, her girlfriends etc. And, according to a drama queen, what *you* have to do is help her with her issues. If she runs out of problems, she goes out and creates new ones. That's because drama queens are addicted to the adrenaline of creating drama. They aren't really happy unless they're in the middle of some great, big, grand production.

> ## what guys want you to know:
>
> *Guys don't kneel at the feet of drama queens. Instead, they run from them ... as fast as they possibly can!*
>
> Secret No. 31

Now some girls can't help but be drama queens. They don't necessarily mean to make drama happen, but they manage to create it anyway. More likely than not, these are girls who desperately want to rid themselves of old, growing-up wounds, only they're clueless as to how to make that happen. For instance, maybe they have an issue with trusting guys because every one of their previous boyfriends cheated on them. Rather than doing some internal detective listening and asking if there's any pattern to the guys they've previously dated, they simply start a new relationship with a guy who reminds them of someone they've dated before. Instead of addressing the problem, they often end up recreating it and hurting themselves again. But in a way, they don't mind getting hurt because, deep down, they feel they deserve the pain and the like the drama.

Whether they choose the crown deliberately or wear it by default, drama queens are not attractive to guys because they're more trouble than being with them is worth. Their stories are not unlike the story of my friend Hannah.

Hannah was a popular girl at her high school. She was fun, outgoing, and made people feel at ease around her. One fall, Hannah returned to classes. But something was different. She was moody and not her bubbly self. She started fights with girls and then called all of her friends to give them a blow-by-blow description of the verbal attacks that had taken place. She texted her friends almost around the clock, asking for help with problems she had. Everywhere she went, she left a wake of upset people. She didn't seem to care anymore about other people's feelings, and the topic of conversation was usually about her latest dramatic encounter with others, including a lot of judgmental gossip.

After a few months into the new school year, Hannah's old friends began to pull away. They were exhausted from dealing with her constant drama. Guys weren't interested in dating her, and Hannah became depressed. She asked one of her remaining friends why no one returned her text messages or IMed her.

Hannah's friend was honest and laid it on the line. She told Hannah that all the drama was pushing people away. Hannah burst into tears.

Hannah confessed that her parents had been fighting all summer and were getting a divorce, and she was scared and sad. She was worried she would hurt one of her parent's feelings if she had to choose which one to live with.

Fortunately, Hannah realized that her reaction to her troubled home life was affecting her behavior around her friends. She vowed to put her tiara to rest and to reach out to friends with concern for their problems, instead of staying stuck in her own. That doesn't mean that Hannah became a doormat, or that she swallowed her pain. She realized everyone has problems and stresses and she began to be available to listen to her friend's problems. In a few months, Hannah's friends came around again. Hannah knows now that she has a tendency toward the dramatic and has to watch herself. But she is happy that she climbed down from the throne and rejoined her friends.

TURN OFF YOUR SPOTLIGHT

Spotlight girls are related to drama queens, but they don't necessarily create drama. What they do is suck all of the oxygen out of a room when they enter, because *everything* has to be about them. They either constantly talk about themselves or act out so that people have to pay attention to them.

Spotlight girls are generally poor listeners. They crash, hijack, and motormouth a great deal. Their favorite topic is themselves. There's no room in that spotlight for anyone else. Who wants to stand next to the spotlight?

A spotlight girl is often working out old growing-up pains or dealing with a huge Itty Bitty Shitty Committee inside her head. Either way, she feels "less than," and putting the spotlight on herself makes her feel important. She may think she needs to stand in the glaring light of a spotlight just to be seen. She may not have a lot of self-confidence and feels she has to show off to make up for her shortcomings. She may need to hear everyone applauding her as she steps onto center stage.

what guys want you to know:

Guys like girls who let their accomplishments and good qualities speak for themselves, rather than drawing attention to themselves or their qualities.

Secret No. 32

If you tend to turn the spotlight on yourself, try to think about the glaring light you're in the next time you flip on the switch. Stop talking about yourself or acting out. Change the topic of conversation over to the guy you're with. Sit down and stop whatever it is you're doing for attention, and instead let the focus be on him.

One way to shine the spotlight on him is to practice detective listening. Everyone loves to talk about themselves, and guys are no different. Learn how to ask the right questions of a guy, just like a good detective, and sit back and let him glow in the light of your complete attention. He will feel appreciated and respected. You will glow in the light of his appreciation. Not only that, you will attract more love and respect from him by giving him the spotlight.

))) What Guys Are Saying About Drama Queens and Spotlight Girls

Oh. My. God. I hate drama queens.
—Tony, USA

Assess the situation around you. Take more than one second. Think of how your words and actions will affect other people. Think before you speak or act!
—Jason, Australia

Get over yourself!
—Josh, USA

Get a life! No one cares about your drama.
—Ariki, New Zealand

Calm down!
—John, USA

Shut up; no one cares!
—Patrick, USA

A girl who needs that much attention, even if she isn't being a drama queen, is too high maintenance for me. I want someone I can feel comfortable with, not someone who constantly needs attention.
—Craig, USA

Spotlight girls are a waste of time. It's all about them. They don't have time for a guy.
—Scott, USA

I run from spotlight girls. They need way too much attention. It's tiring.
—Jay, USA

Dream Girls know that when they sell themselves short, they end up short on respect from guys. Indulging in discount behaviors counts you out as a Dream Girl.

How do you measure up when it comes to discount behaviors? Take a look and see if you need to boost your self-confidence so you can change your behavior to attract more respect and affection. You'll also give yourself a boost in feeling good about yourself.

Here's how Dream girls and just-in-his-jeans girls compare when it comes to discount behaviors:

DREAM GIRLS	JUST-IN-HIS-JEANS GIRLS
• Handle alcohol and drug use wisely and respectfully	• Make "headlines" with their drug or alcohol antics
• Know how to use detective listening to shine the spotlight onto guys	• Believe "it's all about me"
• Are not pinup girls for slutty fashion	• Look like they could be hired as extras in a music video
• Gives up their drama queen tiara so they can help others	• Climb into the throne of drama every day and let everyone know about it
• Work at gaining more self-confidence	• Whine about not being able to change their shortcomings
• Do not pressure guys into drinking or using drugs	• Taunt guys, saying they're geeks if they don't join in and do drugs or drink
• Know they are responsible for fixing their own problems	• Turn to guys to solve their every need
• Do not allow rep-wrecking videos or pictures of themselves to be taken	• Believe that Pam and Paris are home DVD divas

Okay, so now you know what selling yourself short is all about. Now it's time to discuss the big taboo topic that guys want you to know about. Of course, there are other secrets mixed in, too, but keep your eyes open for a shocking revelation that can help you help guys today.

The Reputation Wreckers

Girls are becoming too sexually aggressive. They push guys to have sex and offer us their bodies when we aren't in love with them. It's disturbing. How are we supposed to act? Say "No?" Why don't girls act like ladies anymore?
    –Louis, USA

Girls need to know that guys are confused about sex. We are saturated with it by the media and, honestly, we are overwhelmed trying to figure out what's the right thing to do in today's world. It doesn't help that girls are so easy and on the prowl for sex. Can't girls chill out a little?
    –Jesse, USA

Back in the day, girls were supposed to stay virgins until they married. That didn't mean we always did. I'm just saying that was the expectation. There were "good girls" and there were "bad girls." And the good girls stood a better chance of finding a mate and being respected just by keeping their hymens intact. Even when a girl decided to lose her virginity, she had to act a certain way. Good girls weren't expected to make the first move; that was considered too aggressive, something only bad girls did and most guys didn't like it if they were serious about you being a girlfriend. If you decided to have sex, you at least did so because you were in love with the guy, and you let him take the lead. If a guy wanted to sleep around, or hit on girls, well, that was considered ok. Even expected. The double standard was alive and well back then.

But clearly things have changed. Now girls don't have to be virgins and they can take some first steps in letting a guy know they like him. However, some things are still the same. There is still a double standard, and guys still don't like girls taking a strong lead in sexual activities if they think she is the kind of girl they can love. Even shy guys shared with me that they would like to be the one to make the first move when it comes to sex, even though it was hard for them.

Louis's quote above shows why guys today aren't comfortable with girls being so sexually aggressive. Don't get me wrong: guys still like sex. But like Jesse's quote points out, guys are so saturated with sex in the media and in real life, it's confusing to them. They want girls to chill out, step back, and, well, just slow down. A lot of guys feel it's becoming a bit too crazy out there. They are looking to the girls to help make the world more understandable.

Take oral sex, for instance. Not only are more girls today giving guys blow jobs, but the average age at which girls are indulging in that activity is getting younger and younger. A few decades ago, BJ's were not something you indulged in as casually as girls do today. Hey, guys enjoy that particular activity for sure, but they don't like girls pressuring them into unzipping and they think that girls who give blow jobs to a lot of different guys are just-in-his-jeans girls. Those girls are considered "magic mouths," kinda like the equivalent of a slut.

David, a fourteen year old, reported his experience at the movies. He and his friends sat in the back row, throwing popcorn at each other and having a silly time watching a silly summer movie. One of the girls in the group, changed seats and sat next to him. She asked him if she could give him a blow job. David was totally caught off guard. He was embarrassed to tell his dad about it, but he was so shocked, he needed some advice. He had said "no" to the offer, but was confused as to why a fourteen year old girl he had not known for too long would think it cool to give him a BJ in a public place with his friends all sitting around.

Just because more girls are giving guys BJ's doesn't mean you should, too. Especially once you realize how much damage oral sex can do to your reputation, not to mention that it can open the door to STDs. We'll talk about that—as well as other "discount" sexual behaviors like having a ton of sexual partners and strong-arming guys for sex—in just a second.

RESPECTFUL SEX

Today's society says it's now okay for girls to have sex before marriage, so long as it's "safe" sex. However, what's missing from the equation is the idea of *respectful sex*—sex that is respectful to you and your partner. Respectful sex is the kind of sex that rarely ruins your reputation, your health, or harms your partner in any way. Safe sex is part of respectful sex, and as you know from Health 101, it begins with condoms, condoms, condoms. I think everyone got the memo on that one didn't they? Dream Girls know that safe, respectful sex is the only sex that won't tarnish their Dream Girl crowns.

Of course, not all sex is respectful—especially when it comes to having sex for the first time. Society traditionally thinks of virginity only in terms of girls. We always say that a girl "loses" her virginity or "gives it away," but we never say the same thing whenever a guy loses his. I understand why: for a young woman, losing her virginity is a rite of passage in every sense of the word. But it leaves us with the impression that, when a guy cashes in his V-card, it's no big deal; and that's not at true at all.

In addition, we never think of virginity as something a girl can *take* from a guy; of course, that's not true, either. In fact, some girls seek out male virgins like gunslingers in the Old West. They want to be a guy's first so they can add another notch to their belt, before casting him aside like a used condom. That doesn't sound very respectful, now does it?

The trouble is, most guys don't talk about losing their virginity, so it can be hard for a would-be Dream Girl to understand just how important it is to them. Couple that with the new rules about sex, and a high-tech, high-speed, digital download culture that increasingly objectifies sex while encouraging disrespectful behaviors, and male virginity is another landmine that can easily blow a girl's reputation to bits if she doesn't know the secrets about it.

Remember, sex itself is not wrong or bad. It's the reasons *why* you have sex or how you go about having it that can make sex a problem. With the old guidelines gone, it's more important than ever to understand the sexual behaviors that can derail you on your path to becoming a Dream Girl.

what guys want you to know:

Guys today feel that girls have become way too sexually aggressive. Deep down, guys wish that girls would go back to acting like ladies. That's because deep down, guys would like to go back to being gentlemen.

Secret No. 33

MAKE THE BEST OF THE OL' DOUBLE STANDARD

Of course, when it comes to how society views sex, some things haven't changed at all. If a guy has a lot of sexual partners, he's considered a pimp or a player. If a girl has a lot of sexual partners, she's considered a slut or a whore. It's not really fair that girls get slammed for having sex, and guys don't. That's why it's a called a *double standard*.

When it comes to the consequences of sex, there's also a double standard. If a guy gets a girl pregnant but decides to bail on her, he leaves her with three difficult choices: she can have an abortion if she lives in an area that still allows them (and, depending on which part of the country she lives in, subject herself to further possible disgrace); give birth to the baby, only to put it up for adoption (which, in some cases, can lead to feelings of lifelong guilt or even greater emotional scars for her and her baby); or raise the child on her own, regardless of whether she is emotionally or financially capable of handling that kind of responsibility. Meanwhile, the guy who bailed is off the hook. Not only that, no one knows he is responsible unless the girl names him. There is nothing fair about it, but that's part of the double standard as well. It's the biological reality that women carry the baby, and all the whining about unfairness won't do any good.

So what do you do? Well, if you're a Dream Girl, you make the best of the double standard. And the way to do that is to go back to the point we made earlier about respectful sex. Before you take your clothes off, think about whether you're showing respect to yourself, as well as to the guy you're about to become intimate with. Remember, respectful sex means you and your guy are both willing to face the emotional and biological consequences of having sex. No one gets used or abused.

That's not how Kathy saw sex. There was nothing respectful about it, although she thought she was doing guys a big favor. Kathy loved the way sex felt, and she thought having sex was like giving a guy a gift. She had sex with a lot of guys, but never asked them about their emotional involvement with her. It was just about the pleasure of the act.

She confused a lot of guys. They didn't see her as the bearer of a gift. They eventually just thought of her as a slut. Sorry. That's just the way it is. Many girls, like Kathy, have sex because they like it and think they are doing a big favor for a guy. But having sex with a lot of guys still carries a stigma with it. No matter how much a Dream Girl you may want to be, to guys you're just another just-in-his-jeans girl who likes to sleep around.

> **DR. JENN SAYS...**
>
> *If a Dream Girl decides to have sex, she makes sure it's safe and respectful for her and her partner.*

Guys want to you to make them feel special. They want to believe they're the only one in your universe, because they want you to be the only one in theirs. But it's hard for guys to think that's possible when you hook up with so many others.

Even if the guy you're with is special, can you really expect him to believe he's not just another bang and a bounce when you've had so many sexual partners?

More to the point, the more sexual partners you have, the less special you look in the eyes of that one special guy. "Dr. Jenn it's not fair!" I never said the double standard was fair. I am just telling you what guys told me about the kind of girls they love the most and the kind they don't have much respect for.

(((What Guys Are Saying About Sexual Promiscuity

If a girl has had sex with a lot of guys, it couldn't have meant much to her. If she has sex with me, am I going to mean anything to her, or am I just another fuck to her?
    –Lou, USA

When I look for a girl, I look for someone who does not carry a reputation of being a "whore." As the male in a relationship, dating these girls automatically tags me with a bad reputation. Therefore, I try to stay away from them.
    –Justin, USA

Girls who have slept around make me nervous. I figure they just want to have sex and don't really care about my feelings. If I really like her, how can I know that I am special to her?
    –James, USA

SLOW DOWN, YOU MOVE TOO FAST
(ARE YOU A SPOTTED HYENA?)

Dating has always been about pursuit. Once upon a time, guys always did the pursuing, but gradually that changed. And that's a good thing. After all, some guys are shy about asking girls out, so they appreciate it when girls take the initiative. The problem is when you act too fast and take your pursuit beyond the point of respect. That's certainly what's happening with a lot of girls today. Some girls today have become downright predatory, like a spotted hyena ready to attack.

Spotted hyenas are an interesting species. The females are larger than the males and are more dominant. Not only that, they have a phallus that can engorge and look like an erect penis. Being the more aggressive of the sexes, the female spotted hyena can easily intimidate her male counterparts by flashing her pseudo erection. Obviously, human females do not have the same physical capability as the female spotted hyena. Yet some girls act as if they've grown a penis and that gives guys the heebie-jeebies.

what guys want you to know:

Guys like fast cars.
They don't like fast girls.

Secret No. 34

Don't care for that metaphor? Okay. Let's try this one: Guys like fast cars, not fast girls.

When a guy wants a relationship, he wants to be the one who chases you, not the other way around. Girls who act like race horses out of the gate, heading straight toward the finish line of a guy's zipper, lose a guy's respect.

That's what happened to a girl named Crystal.

Crystal walked up to a hot guy at a high school football game and introduced herself. Within a few minutes, she was bragging about her past conquests and asked if he wanted to hook up after the football game. She was surprised that he said no.

"Don't all guys just want sex?" she asked her friend, Sue, after the game.

"No, girl, they don't," Sue told her. "Not every guy is gonna move on you just because you want him to."

A few weeks later, Crystal heard that the guy she had approached actually had a crush on her before she opened her mouth and asked him to get it on. She felt bad about turning him off and started wondering whether maybe she was getting a bad rep. When she asked Sue about it, she was surprised to learn that most of the guys in school considered her a just-in-his-jeans girl. Guys didn't see her as girlfriend material because they thought she only wanted sex.

Learning the truth hurt Crystal, but sometimes that's what it takes. She told Sue she was going to do some soul searching and figure out why she was so quick to jump a guy.

If you have sex with a guy right away or expect him to have sex with you right away, the message you're sending is that you don't want to take the time or effort to really get to know him. That's because sex, as close as it can bring two people together, can also be a barrier to intimacy. It's usually awkward to go backward and get to know someone once you've had sex. It's as if you jumped right into the middle of a movie without knowing what the story was about. You have to stop and hit the rewind button to figure out where it's going.

Think about the last time a guy played every card in his "I-gotta-get-laid" hand to try to hook up with you. Did you feel disrespected that he only wanted your body and had little if any regard for you as a person? Well, that's exactly how many guys feel when you move in on them. They may be flattered that you find them sexually appealing, but they want to be thought of as more than just a body part.

Of course, not all girls and not all guys will care; for some, sex will be enough. But the majority of the guys interviewed said that they didn't like being seen only as a means for a girl to get her freak on.

NO MEANS NO, NO MATTER WHO SAYS IT

Guys also complain about girls who strong-arm them for sex. It is really confusing. Of course, given how prevalent sex is in today's instant access culture, where images of women seducing men are available in all forms of media 24/7, it's no wonder girls feel that they should make a guy jump into bed at the snap of their fingers, whether he's ready for it or not.

But before you decide to flex your muscles and put the moves on a guy, remember this: "no" means no, whether you say it or he does. Just

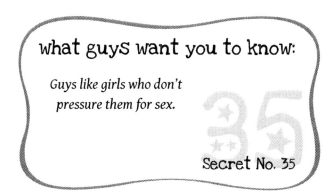

what guys want you to know:

Guys like girls who don't pressure them for sex.

Secret No. 35

like it's wrong for a guy to pressure you into any sexual activity you don't want to engage in, it's wrong for you to do the same to a guy. You may think you're turning him on by telling him how good you can make him feel, but when you keep at it once he's told you he doesn't want sex, you're stepping over the line of respect.

Look at this way. Guys go through far more mental gymnastics than girls do when they feel pressured to have sex. For one, they feel confused because, as guys, they feel they have to say "yes." For better or worse, that is the stereotype: guys want sex. Even if guys know that isn't true, they often feel compelled to comply because our culture expects them to behave like a raging sex machine. And besides, if he doesn't comply, that can bring on even more pressure than you demanding sex. For example, if his friends hear that he turned down sex, will they tease him? Will they think he is gay? Is he somehow less than a man?

With girls, it's a lot different. For the most part, girls don't have to worry about what their friends will think of them if they say no. Although the media and our culture tell girls it's perfectly fine to be the pursuer, guys still expect girls to be the ones to say no. But when you switch roles and pressure guys into having sex with you, it not only disrespects the guy, it makes you look like the spotted hyena, aggressive and acting masculine—not the most attractive picture!

So why do girls pressure guys into having sex? With some girls, it could be that they're just really horny or lonely, maybe even bored. In some cases, however, it's because they need a lot of reassurance that they are attractive to a guy. Or they may think that if they can get a guy to have sex with them the guy will then fall in love with them.

Even if you have mad sex skills and are an absolute freak in the sheets, if you want to be a Dream Girl, know that strong-arming a guy into having sex won't make him like or love you more. It'll only hurt your reputation by making you seem like a just-in-his-jeans girl.

The next time you find yourself pressuring a guy into having sex, ask yourself what need is the sex going to fill? Are you simply hot and bothered? Are you hoping the sex will make you feel more loved or more attractive? Are you trying to connect with another human being and not feel so alone or lonely? Is there a way you can meet your needs that doesn't involve strong-arm tactics?

If you think back to your answers to the growing-up pains quiz in Chapter One, you might find some reasons why you feel the need to pressure a guy for sex. If old wounds are making you force a guy into sex, how might you begin to heal those wounds? It's a big question, so take some time to think about the answer.

 *How might I begin to heal the wounds?*

One other thing to note: inviting guys to hook up with you by snapping naked pictures of yourself, or shooting steamy videos and sending them over the internet via your cell or computer is not the way to get a guy's respect. You'll get his attention for sure. And you might get the attention of some law enforcement personnel as well. It's illegal to send naked or sexually explicit pictures of anyone under the age of eighteen to someone else. The new trend of getting to know guys by sending out sexual pictures of yourself is simply not a good idea for lots of reasons.

Remember that every email, every IM you send gets saved for all eternity in some vast memory system of the company you use to transmit your information. Information you share now can come back and haunt you years down the road. So share safely. Ok?

Let's let the guys have a say about girls and hooking up right away:

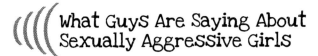

What Guys Are Saying About Sexually Aggressive Girls

I lose respect for a girl if she wants to hook up right away. She isn't looking for a real relationship if she wants sex so fast.
  –Tim, Australia

I feel insecure wondering why a girl would want to hook up with me right away.
  –Nick, USA

Hooking up with a girl right away would tell me that she has probably done the same thing before and will do it again.
  –Joshua, USA

I like a girl that gives things time and moves slow. I would like to get to know the girl really well before we make the decision to hook up.
  –Chris, USA

Being pressured by a girl to have sex made me feel like she didn't care about my feelings.
    –Heath, Australia

Some girls can be too sexually aggressive. For awhile, the only thing my girlfriend wanted to do was to have sex. For awhile, it made me feel good as if someone wanted me, but it also made me feel that's all she wanted. That didn't feel good!
    –Travis, USA

After being pressured by a girl to have sex, I felt awkward. It wasn't intercourse; she wanted me to masturbate her. It felt really bad. Here she was, begging me to ... and I knew that if I didn't, she would get incredibly upset and get ideas that I didn't like her or that I didn't find her attractive.
    –Avrom, Australia

Some girls think that if they pressure a guy into having sex, he will stay with them and won't be interested in any other girls. But if I have hit it already, I am not that interested in hitting it again. I will look for another girl. No guy wants to be pressured into having sex.
    –Shane, USA

A girl once took me home with her when I was really drunk and pressured me into sex. I felt so dirty, gross, and used afterward. I didn't know her at all, and I really wasn't into it when I was sober. Anybody that feels they need to pressure others into having sex needs a clue and [needs to] learn that some people are not here just to provide others pleasure.
    –Shawn, USA

ORAL SEX IS STILL SEX

Most of the girls and guys interviewed for this book said they did not consider oral sex to be sex. This attitude has become pretty common in our society over the last decade or so. Maybe that's because we once had a president who, in explaining what he was doing with a certain young intern who was down on her knees performing oral sex on him under his big desk in the oval office, insisted that he "did not have sex with that woman." Who knows how this perception came about, and, for that matter, who cares? It doesn't change the fact that oral sex is still a type of sex. It may not be intercourse, but it gets you to the same place that intercourse takes you. You have an orgasm. That's sex.

In today's world, oral sex is given as currency to attract a guy's attention. With so many lyrics touting the necessity of women getting on their knees to please a man, it's no wonder that oral sex seems almost automatic.

Recently, I stood in line at the local fast-food joint, giving in to my craving for french fries. Two teen girls stood in line in front of me. One was twirling her long, brown hair between her fingers. I couldn't help but overhear her sighing, "He just *has* to like me! What do I do to get him to like me?"

Her friend was busy texting someone on her phone. She didn't even bother looking up from the keypad. She simply said, "Blow him."

"Oooooh ... yeah, they all go for that!" the first girl tittered. She even stopped twirling her hair, apparently convinced she now knew exactly what to do to win her crush's heart.

Hearing her friend's advice made me sad. I wanted to tap Hair Twirling Girl on the shoulder and tell her that, while her friend's advice might get her into that guy's pants, it wouldn't help her a bit if she wanted to get into his heart. And that's the ultimate destination, isn't it? I would hope she wanted to get loved, not just laid.

A generation ago, oral sex was something special—the icing on the cake, so to speak. Now it is almost as perfunctory as a hello. But performing oral sex on a lot of different guys doesn't win you anything except a wrecked reputation ... and worse. Read on.

Most guys will never ask a girl how many blow jobs she's given. On the other hand, they consider girls who perform oral sex with a lot of guys, (even the girls who are still technically virgins) to be "magic mouths"— the equivalent of a bed-hopping slut. Once you get the reputation of being a magic mouth, you might as well write it with a Sharpie across your forehead. Being perceived as a magic mouth is one image that's almost impossible for a girl to erase.

And of course, there are health issues. No, you can't get pregnant from oral sex, but you can still get an STD. Gonorrhea of the throat is not pretty, ladies! And AIDS is still infecting people; not to mention the HPV virus is now linked to throat cancer. Yuck!

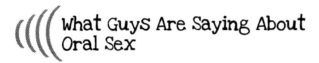

What Guys Are Saying About Oral Sex

Sex is sex no matter what word you put in front of it. Even if the girl is a virgin and gives a lot of blow jobs to random guys, it would lower my respect for her.
   –Tim, Australia

In my opinion, I respect females less when they give BJs to a lot of guys. In a way, there is a similar viewpoint with comparing sluts to magic mouths. I respect females who have class, who have confidence about themselves.
   –Ty, USA

If I were to find out the girl I had been dating hadn't slept around too much but was a "magic mouth," it would definitely make me raise an eyebrow about who I'm with.
   –Jake, USA

SUFFERING IN SILENCE: MALE VIRGINITY

Why do Dream Girls need to understand male virginity? Because the topic is taboo. If we talk about it at all, we usually make fun of it, like we do of the character Jim in the movie *American Pie*. You remember Jim: he's a high school senior who's very smart; he's got a loving dad and a bright future ahead of him. But because Jim is still a virgin, all his friends think he's a loser. They make fun of him.

The problem with this stereotype is that many guys really *do* care who they lose their virginity to. Male virginity is no laughing matter. But because guys don't feel comfortable talking about it, nobody understands it. That's when the myths and misconceptions about male virginity can trip you up on the road to becoming a Dream Girl. And unless you know the facts, girls, it's way too easy to make the mistakes that could rule you out of a guy's heart.

There are a growing number of girls who sniff out male virgins. They couldn't care less about the guy's feelings. They figure if a guy's still a virgin, he can't wait to "bust it" so that he can officially join the "real men" club. They assume he's just another guy who can't wait to have sex, that he won't think about them once it's over—and that they're doing him a big favor. After all, he's just a guy, and all guys are the same. He's just another raging sex machine waiting to be revved up, right?

Wrong. Some guys may want to cash in their V-card as soon as they can but certainly not all of them. Some guys, in fact, feel intense regret, sorrow, guilt, or shame after losing their virginity. Those feelings can intensify should a guy realize that the girl who popped his cherry sees him as just another notch on her belt, like it was no big deal. Girls who are cavalier about a guy's virginity are just as shady as guys who treat girls the same way.

What Guys Are Saying About Male Virginity

Girls and society in general don't understand male virginity because if you are a still a virgin at twenty, you are considered a weirdo.
  –Aaron, Australia

No, women don't understand male virginity. Guys certainly don't talk about it. Women don't know anything about it outside of teen movies, which are often inaccurate and misleading ... No, I don't think that society understands male virginity. It's one of the least discussed topics.
  –Harry, USA

I think the decision to lose your virginity is a very personal one. No one should feel pressured to give up something that is precious to them before they are truly ready. I don't think that girls understand male virginity at all. There is a lot of pressure exerted by our friends that we would never tell them about. It is a big deal to guys as well—we don't want to feel left out of the big boys club. Society doesn't understand male virginity. I even know of guys who can't really remember theirs because they lied about it and said they had lost it before they actually did, just to fit in. The lie became the reality.
    –Paul, New Zealand

When I lost my virginity, I really regretted it, because I didn't feel the least bit of affection toward her. She just wanted to know what it felt like, so we went to my grandparents' house and ended up cuddling and so on.
    –Caleb, USA

I've never had sex, although the temptation is still there. I don't want to lose my virginity with just any passing girl. It represents a serious step for me, so I'm hoping to keep it until I find the only one special girl [who] I can give it to. My friends used to taunt me, tell me I'm gay or something like that if [they] knew that I was still a virgin. That's the reason I never really talk about it. I like some girls, but I seriously wouldn't want to hurry things up— they would think that I'm just looking for sex, which isn't the case. You have to really know someone to have a long-term relationship with them.
    –Zaki, Algeria

When I was pressured into having sex, it made me feel dirty. The girl ended up going back to her boyfriend.
    –Jim, USA

Most girls do not understand male virginity. Girls must understand, when a guy is a virgin, he doesn't know anything about sex. The women I've been around expected a guy to know instinctively what to do as if it is impressed in our genes. Girls need to understand that our first time, we are very nervous, and it might not even work.

    –Joe, USA

I don't think anyone understands anything about male virginity. It's a tough topic. We don't talk much about [it] with anyone. We just know when it's gone.

    –Neil, Canada

what guys want you to know:

Dream Girls respect virginity, whether it is their virginity or his. They don't give it away, and they don't take it away casually. They know and respect that the heart has a say in the matter. They listen for what the heart has to say.

Secret No. 36

The classic stereotype is that all male virgins are like Jim: they don't care who they lose it to or how it takes place. They just want to have sex. The problem with this stereotype is that it makes holding out tough for the guys who do care.

The fact is, many guys experience regret or other intense, negative feelings after losing their virginity. But because they're "not supposed to" feel that way—after all, "real men" don't talk about that kind of stuff— they end up suffering in silence. They don't feel they can trust anyone to share their feelings with. They're afraid that they'll be ridiculed.

"I can't tell my friends I regret I lost my virginity to the wrong girl, and now I am bummed out about it," a guy named Tony told me. "Are you kidding me? They'd laugh their asses off and tell me I was being a big pussy."

Tony's not alone in his plight. Why? It goes back to the classic stereotype. Most people can't imagine a guy ever worrying about losing his virginity too soon. They assume he should be happy to be rid of the stigma of being a virgin.

What Guys Are Saying About the Challenges of Male Virginity

Being a virgin at nineteen is hard; I'm not going to lie. It's a lot of pressure from others to have sex. It's not that they are directly pressuring, but it's like an "everyone else has done it, why haven't I?" kind of thing. I am glad I haven't slept with twenty-something girls like one of my friends, and he is only twenty. Gross. Ya know? I am waiting for the right time.
    –Mike, USA

Most girls think that guys are just waiting for any girl to lose it to. And for me, that isn't true. I will wait for sure until I love the girl and she loves me back.
    –Carlos, USA

People don't understand male virginity. In the new generation, kids pretend they aren't virgins. Being a "V" isn't cool anymore, so they feel they will be ridiculed by their friends.
    –Mike, USA

If girls think we don't care about our virginity, they are wrong. Men do care about their virginity; it's not a joke to us, and if society sees it that way, then they are wrong!
    –Bede, England

EVEN PARENTS DON'T ALWAYS UNDERSTAND

We talked before about some of the double standards in our culture's views on sex. There's definitely a double standard when it comes to the subject of virginity. Most parents recognize that their daughter's first time is a special event: one that should be approached carefully, not casually. They know how vulnerable their girl can be at that moment, so they take every precaution to shield her from emotional or physical harm. The problem is, most parents don't put anywhere near the same amount of emphasis on virginity when it comes to protecting their sons.

Some parents today don't understand that their sons can be every bit as vulnerable as their daughters—emotionally, as well as physically—when engaging in sex for the very first time. Sure, they may sit their sons down for the inevitable "sex talk," but they rarely discuss the emotions that emerge during one's first time, as they would with their daughters. For some reason, they just assume their boys are ready. Some parents even so go far as hiring a prostitute or setting their virginal sons up with an older woman to "break them in" or simply to "get it over with."

One Texas father of two teenage boys told me he believed that any guy who whines or cries about losing his virginity is probably gay. He said, "They are too in touch with their feminine side, and I bet a few years from now they will come out of the closet." With this type of mentality, it's no wonder so many guys—and girls—have such a hard time talking about male virginity, let alone understanding it.

Dream Girls handle virginal guys with extreme care. That doesn't mean you have to walk on eggshells or treat them like they were made of glass. It does, however, mean treating them with respect. Dream Girls know that a guy can be every bit as vulnerable as they are (or were) when they have sex for the first time. Dream Girls also know that the first time should be special. So make sure your motives for hooking up with him aren't selfish.

> **DR. JENN SAYS...**
>
> *Male virginity is a tender topic that guys want to be able to talk about. Understanding male virginity begins with the word* respect.

"I've always wanted to take a guy's virginity," a girl named Maureen told me. "There is some kind of power in it, you know? It was thrilling to know I was his first—I knew he would remember me the rest of his life. I really loved him, and we talked about it before. I made sure he was ready. I didn't assume that just because I was willing that he was too. We have been together for a few years now."

Maureen knew it was a fantasy of hers to be with a virgin, but she made really sure the guy she hooked up with wanted to lose his virginity—and that she would respect him afterward. She checked her ego at the door, like a Dream Girl should.

If you are thinking of having sex with a virgin, don't just jump right in. Test the waters first, because once you take the plunge, you can't stop, go back, and undo it. Talk to him first, listen to his feelings, be clear on his expectations (and ensure that's he's clear about yours), and above all, be safe. Make sure he's wearing a condom. If he has religious issues, be straight about those. Ask whether he'll regret giving you his virginity—and pay attention to his answer. If he hesitates in any way at all, it's time for you to stop moving forward.

Remember, Dream Girls know that "no" means no as much for him as it does for you. If he says "no," that doesn't mean he wants you to keep on trying to seduce him until he says, "yes." Nor does it mean he's rejecting you. All it means is that he isn't ready for sex right there and then. Respect his "no," and he'll respect you for respecting him.

Respecting his "no" also requires that you skip the trip to the gossip vineyard and tell all your girlfriends that he won't put out. Dream Girls respect a guy's privacy and dignity. So issue a gossip gag order on yourself.

That same gag order should also be in effect even if he says "yes."

The stereotype is that guys can't wait to blab about who they do it with. But as we saw in Chapter Four, girls today share way more sexual secrets than guys do. Dream Girls know it's disrespectful to kiss and tell, so they keep the details about their private life private.

If you are still a virgin, it's important to ask yourself if you are ready for a sexual relationship and all the physical and emotional responsibilities that come with it. Dream Girls respect themselves and stay true to themselves. Be as careful in dealing with your own virginity as you would in dealing with a guy's.

Two virgins giving themselves to each other is a romantic ideal, but make sure the reality of the situation matches your romantic notion. Your heart and his are both vulnerable. So listen to yourself as well. If you are still a virgin and your guy isn't, be true to yourself if you want to keep your virginity, even if he wants you to give it to him. You're self esteem is more important than his sex drive!

I've mentioned that a growing number of girls like to pop guys' cherries for the pure sport of it. They call it "collecting V-cards." A girl has sex with as many virgins as she can, each time adding a new card to her collection, and then brags to her friends about how many virgins she's bagged. Girls who collect V-cards no doubt believe in the stereotype that all guys want to lose their virginity and don't care who they do it with. It never dawns on them that they might be scarring the guy for life.

There are many reasons why certain girls end up becoming V-card collectors. They may have been abused themselves as virgins, so they prey on guys to settle the score. Some do it because they crave attention, while others do it because they're hooked on the power trip it brings. No matter what the collector's motivation, guys look at them all the same. V-card collectors are not worthy of a guy's respect.

I was at a party and had too much to drink. Some of the people there knew I was still a virgin. We were in the kitchen, and one of the girls pulled off my pants and made me get a hard-on and had sex with me. She took advantage of me. Everyone in the kitchen watched. Some even took pictures with their cell phones. They showed me the pictures the next day. I was so embarrassed. I don't remember a lot of it. But I regret I lost my virginity like that. I feel really bad. I didn't want it to be that way. The girl involved had no right to take advantage of me. I know we were drinking, but I should have been safe with my buddies.
    –Steven, USA

What happened to Steven is a form of rape. We have a double standard about rape, too, that says it can never happen to a guy; after all, a hard-on means "yes," right?

Wrong again, girls. You can rape a guy. All an erection means is that a guy's body is physically turned on. It does not indicate in any way whether his heart or mind wants sex or that he has said "yes" to your advances.

Girls who take sexual advantage of guys are not respected and will never come close to wearing the crown of a Dream Girl. Respect is a small thing to lose when you consider that taking advantage of a guy is criminal, and you can be brought up on charges just like a guy can be.

Guys who lose their virginity and regret it are left with physical and emotional scars resulting from the pain and regret of losing their virginity. Some of the physical scars come from guys turning to self-mutilation or "cutting" to release the pain of losing their virginity. Usually girls are more prone to cutting; however, some of the guys I interviewed said they cut themselves in response to losing their virginity to the wrong girl.

ONE GUY'S SONG OF DESPAIR

One of the earliest bands on MySpace is Hollywood Undead. People love this band because the music speaks to them. Here are part of the lyrics of a Hollywood Undead song that really captures the anguish of guys who cut themselves because of being emotionally hurt by a girl: (and, if you know the song, the girl didn't up too well either.)

I've, been abused, I feel so used, because of you
I'm sorry oh
I'm sorry no
I wish I could have quit you.
I wish I never missed you,
And told you that I loved you, every time I fucked you.
The future that we both drew, and all the shit we've been through.
Obsessed with the thought of you, the pain just grew and grew!
How could you do this to me?

Look at what I made for you,
it never was enough
and the world
is what I gave to you.
I used to be love struck; now I'm just fucked up.
Pull up my sleeves and see the patterns of my cuts!

From "My Black Dahlia,"
Hollywood Undead
Copyright © 2006 Interscope Records.
Used with permission.

Here is one guy's story about self mutilating after he lost his virginity.

Well, I have to say that I was very trusting before this girl hap-
pened. As I sit here and think about it, I was stupid for wanting
to have sex so fast. I should have waited because I had no idea
what I was in for. She had no respect for me. I was used. I hate it
so much that it happened. Up until about a year after I gave her
my virginity, I was a mess mentally. All I could think about was
what I did wrong. Why was I with someone like that in the first
place? She changed from being so sweet and cute to being like
she didn't care about me. I didn't cope well with it after I found
out she cheated on me. My first feelings of love were actually just
imagined in my head. I felt so bad, I took screws, broken glass,
and razors and cut myself on my arm and face and chest. I didn't
want the pain to just be in my head. I wanted to feel it as well,
to let it out somehow. I had no one to talk to about that kind of
stuff. I had to work things out in my own head, and it took a very
long time to recover. In the end, it was a horrible nightmare, and
I realized I had lost my virginity to the wrong person.
–Anthony, USA

)))) What Guys Are Saying About Losing Their Virginity

I was pressured by my girlfriend to have sex with her all the time. I finally gave in and lost my virginity to her, and I've regretted it every day since. I was waiting for a special girl and a special time, and it definitely wasn't special. I felt used, and I felt I had abandoned my own morals and beliefs. I let myself down. I felt ashamed of myself that I gave in to her pressuring me. I do not think she respected me very much. I felt like she used me. After that, she thought I would give in and have sex with her any time she wanted. And she wasn't even concerned with how it was for me as long as she got what she wanted.

Girls don't think a guy's virginity is as important as a girl's. Girls take it for granted and think that we are the one who should wait for them. They think we don't deserve someone who will wait for us until we are ready. People in general have double standards. They think if a guy is still a virgin, he is less than a man. It puts a lot of pressure on the guys who wait.

–Kenny, USA

I don't think people understand the issues of male virginity. I didn't care at the time when I lost mine, but later I regretted it. We started arguing right afterward, and we couldn't stop the fights. It destroyed our relationship.

–Jason, USA

I was in the fifth grade, and my older cousin made me and a girl have sex. I felt raped. I wish I had held onto my virginity longer. You should lose it to someone you will always love and be friends with.

–Devon, USA

Losing my virginity was a bad move because the feelings took

longer to go away than the night with her.
   –Bryan, USA

When I lost my virginity, it wasn't special. It was a random hookup, and I really feel bad about that. I still regret not waiting, but at the time there was so much pressure from TV and society to lose it, and I gave in.
   –Harry, USA

Girls put a lot of pressure on a guy, more than I think they realize. We have very fragile egos, and it's probably a lot easier to coerce us than it is to coerce a girl. The results are the same; we feel used, but we are just forced to hide our baggage.
   –Joshua, USA

I lost my virginity when I was very young to a girl who was five years older than me. After it happened, I was a different person. She and I stopped talking, and it was very awkward every time I saw her.
   –James, USA

I lost my virginity in a one-night stand to a girl who had just broken up with her boyfriend. I felt terrible. I'm not a bad guy in life, but I felt like such a bad person afterward. I wasn't treated well afterward, either. The next day she got a new boyfriend. In my opinion, it's okay to be a virgin. Never feel pressured to lose it.
   –Robert, England

Here's one guy's story of losing his virginity and the long-term ramifications that single act had in his life:

I didn't lose my virginity until the Monday after spring break of my senior year in high school. But let me tell you the story up until that night. I lived in New York for my eighth and ninth grades. My first love, Christine, lived down the street. We "dated" both years. After the ninth grade, my father, who was in the Navy, was reassigned to California. Christine and I kept in touch for the next three years, writing, e-mailing, etc. Our plan the whole time was to lose our virginity together [during] spring break of our senior year.

I saved up enough money and bought my own plane ticket to fly out to see her. I was supposed to fly out Saturday morning, but the day before, she called me and told me she got drunk at a party. She lost her virginity to some random guy in the back seat of her car. I was crushed, to say the least. I ended up going to New York as planned and spent the week with some of my old friends and refused to see her or talk to her.

When I got back to California, my aunt and uncle asked me to babysit my cousin and one of his friends. When the friend's mom came to pick him up, I talked to her for a while, and she gave me her phone number. She was twenty-six, and I had just turned eighteen. I ended up calling her that night, and she invited me out with her and some of her friends. I met up with them later. During the night, she got drunk. I drove her home, and she invited me up. Fill in the details from there. After I gave her my virginity, she told me I had to leave. I never talked to her again.

A young, heartbroken, and hormonally-charged eighteen-year-old made a dumb mistake. I still regret it to this day. I think what hurt the most was the compounding of having my heart broken by my first love, Christine, saving something so special for her, then giving it away to a stranger who rejected me, too. I spent many years just sleeping with whoever would say yes after that, no matter how pretty, ugly, fat, skinny, whatever, just to try to find the feeling of giving someone something that special. Unfortunately, no matter how many women come and go, I don't think it will ever be the same.

–Josh, USA

WHERE TO BEGIN?

Dream Girls educate themselves about things they don't understand. So start by asking questions. Become curious about this taboo topic of male virginity. Begin a conversation with a guy you know and trust, and see what he has to say about the topic. Use all of your detective listening skills. Perhaps the key to changing the stereotype of young men as just raging sex machines is through honest, trusting conversations. If enough Dream Girls get the conversation with guys started, the truth about male virginity has a chance to be heard.

So there's a lot to think about the next time you reach for his zipper. Guys aren't all horn dogs who want sex. If you want to be a true Dream Girl, you need to think about how you can make any sexual activity you decide to engage in be safe and respectful for both you and your partner. And you certainly won't pressure a guy into sex or collect V-cards or become a magic mouth. Respect has to flow through all areas of your life. You can't leave it at the bedroom door or in the back seat of a car.

If you have decided that sex isn't right for you right now, know that you aren't alone. Even though it seems that everyone is doing it, that's not totally true. Respect your own boundaries and honor yourself. As much as guys don't want you to pressure them into having sex, I certainly don't want you to feel pressured that you have to give into society's new accepting view of sex, sex, and more sex. Know your boundaries and be respectful of guys' boundaries. With that in mind, you will be well on your way to getting the love and respect you want.

Let's compare Dream Girls and just-in-his-jeans girls with regard to sexual activities. See how many behaviors you have in common with the Dream Girl side of the column.

DREAM GIRLS	JUST-IN-HIS-JEANS GIRLS
• Never pressure a guy for sex	• Use strong arm tactics to get laid
• Respect that a guy is more than just his genitals	• Use a guy to get off and don't care about his feelings

• Handle virgins with kid gloves	• Collect V-cards for the fun of it
• Know that being a magic mouth is a reputation wrecker	• Perform a lot of oral sex without knowing or caring that their behavior is the equivalent of being a slut to most guys
• Understand male virginity is a taboo topic	• Haven't the slightest clue about male virginity
• Do not use sex to get love	• Believe sex makes a guy fall in love
• Keep their sexual activity away from the gossip vineyard	• Spread their sexual news through the grapevine for all to hear
• Listen to a guy's heart, not just what's in his pants	• Thinks an erection means yes to sex
• Respect their own sexual boundaries	• Have never given much thought to their own beliefs about sex for herself
Write your own ideas here:	**Write your own ideas here:**

Remember, it's not just virgins who Dream Girls treat with dignity and respect. They treat all guys that way. Dream Girls don't strong-arm for sex; and they do not kiss and tell. They know that guys want them to act like ladies so they can begin to act more like gentlemen. Moreover, Dream Girls know that guys want them to learn a really big lesson that can help guys be better men. They want girls to learn how to ... well, read the next chapter and see for yourself.

Let Go and Forgive

"Girls don't know how to forgive. Even when they say they have forgiven you, they throw things in your face that you did months or even years ago. They hold onto every little thing."
–Mark, USA

Forgiveness is a uniquely human ability that Dream Girls practice with abundance, both toward others *and* toward themselves. What does a Dream Girl do when someone hurts her? She acknowledges she has been hurt, works through her hurt feelings or pain, and then chooses to forgive. She wipes the slate clean and doesn't bring the issue up again with the person who did her dirty. In other words, Dream Girls *forgive for good.*

"You have got to be kidding, Dr. Jenn. You actually want me to forgive the jerks and bitches who make my life miserable?"

Yes, I do. I realize that can be challenging sometimes, but I also know you can do it because I know you want to be loved and respected. You've got to forgive, *really forgive*, if you want to be really loved.

As I say, everyone makes mistakes—you and I included. Those "jerks" and "bitches" you refer to ... well, those are just labels you put on someone. Remember, when we slap negative labels onto people (or create enemy images out of them), we no longer see them as human beings but, rather, merely as things. That's when compassion walks right out of the door. If you cannot see the humanity in another person, then please, do a U-turn and look again. He or she is no different than you, even if it doesn't seem that way.

None of us are without fault. All of us need forgiveness at one time or another.

You can either forgive the people who wrong you, or you can hold onto your resentment and anger and let it slowly eat away at you. The choice is yours.

Just be aware that guys see girls who do not learn how to forgive as just-in-his-jeans girls. Why? Because girls who can't forgive can be the biggest gossipers, bullies, cheaters, liars, drama queens, spotlight girls, and senders of nasty messages. They act out their hate and anger, whereas girls who learn how to practice forgiveness, have no need to pay back anyone. This is so important I am going to say it again: Girls who do not know how to forgive can be the biggest gossipers, bullies, cheaters, liars, and drama queens—just-in-his-jeans girls.

Maybe Matt Groening, the creator of *The Simpsons*, has dealt with an unforgiving woman In his life. In a scene from *The Simpson Movie*, Lisa hits Homer in the stomach, crying, "I hate you."

Marge makes her stop.

Lisa whimpers, "But I am so angry."

Marge says matter-of-factly, "You're a woman; you can hold onto it forever."

The scene gets a lot of laughs, and not just from guys.

When I interviewed guys about what secrets they wish girls knew about forgiveness, they said they don't feel as if girls know *how* to forgive. They grumbled that even when a girl claims she has forgiven, she is quick to throw old mistakes in their faces, which means she hasn't learned how to forgive at all.

Quick story: There once was a Tibetan monk who was imprisoned and tortured at the hands of his Chinese captors. When the monk was finally released, he was interviewed about his ordeal. When asked if he was ever afraid, he nodded and answered, "Oh, yes, every day. I was afraid I would lose my compassion for the guards who tortured me."

what guys want you to know:

Guys want you to learn how to forgive.

Secret No. 37

Bonus Secret

Even if someone isn't sorry for what he or she did to you, and you offer him or her forgiveness anyway, you rock. That makes you a very special type of Dream Girl who guys will adore because it shows them that you have compassion.

Compassion is the foundation not only of forgiveness but also of being a Dream Girl. Compassion means that when you see someone suffering, you identify with his or her suffering and want to help.

People who hurt others you usually do so because they are acting out old growing-up wounds and suffering. When you look beyond their actions and see that they are hurting, you'll find yourself more able to pardon the wrong they did to you and extend forgiveness to them.

Of course, few of us will reach the level of enlightenment of the jailed Tibetan monk, but that shouldn't stop us from trying. When you have compassion for everyone, as the monk did, there is little to forgive because you understand that people are not perfect.

STEP RIGHT UP TO FORGIVENESS

Okay, learning how to forgive is a challenging topic. So let's back up for a moment and define forgiveness.

Forgiveness means we not only pardon someone whose actions have harmed us, but we also let go of our anger or resentment towards them. We don't retaliate. Instead of wearing our hurt like a badge of honor, we *put aside our hurt or disappointment and move on.*

This isn't to say we should turn a blind eye to all wrongdoing. The world wouldn't function very well if we let people who do really bad things roam the streets. Nor am I suggesting that justice gets lost in the forgiveness process. Retaliation is the payback of harm with harm, while justice is the legal administration of a set punishment. Dream Girls don't retaliate.

The first step in learning about how to forgive is to *acknowledge that you have been hurt.* That seems fairly straightforward now, wouldn't you say? If you don't know you have been harmed, there isn't anything to forgive.

Step two is to *own what you feel.* Don't try to talk yourself out of your feelings or ignore them. That simply is not healthy. Remember the point we talked about in Chapter Three about deciding what's true for you? The same thing applies here. Make sure you know what's true for you when you have been hurt. If you feel like screaming at the top of your lungs, banging your head against the wall, or smashing something to pieces, then so be it. Feel your feelings—just make sure you don't *act out* your feelings if doing so will cause you to harm yourself or someone else in any way. Sit with your emotions for a few days. Then after that, let them go.

Of course, if what happened to you is a big, traumatic event, then obviously it will take more than a few days to work through it. Take as much time as you need to process your feelings to the point where you're ready to move on.

"You make it sound so easy, Dr. Jenn. How do you just let go of your feelings?"

It's not easy. You have to be willing to let go, and you need to practice learning how to do that. But you can do it. I'll show you some ways to do it in just a minute.

The third step in forgiving is to actually *forgive*. It sounds silly, but you have to really mean it—acknowledge to yourself that you are actually forgiving someone.

There now. Three steps. I know you can master them.

FORGET AND FORGIVE

I'm sure you've heard the old saying, "Forgive and forget." While there's certainly a lot of truth to that, it's really the other way around. We have to learn to let go first before we're ready to forgive.

That's why step two is the one most people get stuck on. They sit on their feelings a long time and ruminate over what people have done to them.

But if you keep thinking about how much you didn't deserve what happened to you—and let's face it, most likely you didn't deserve what happened to you—and you hold on to your hurt or carry a grudge, you can't forgive and move on. Part of moving on is forgetting about the past and being in the present moment, where the real juice and joy of life is.

Here's another quick story about Tibetan monks that illustrates our point. (Now don't worry; I'm not "going spiritual" on you. Nor do I expect you to run off and join a monastery or convent or anything like that. It's just that Eastern philosophy, which is where these stories originate, includes many writings on forgiveness that really hit the nail on the head. Perhaps that's why these teachings have lasted for thousands and thousands of years.)

An old monk went out for a long walk with a new young monk. The young monk deeply respected the old monk and watched him carefully, learning how to do everything properly at the monastery. Both monks had taken a vow of chastity, along with a vow to never touch a woman's flesh in any manner. No handshakes, no hugs—you get the picture.

About an hour into their walk, the pair came upon a woman in a wedding gown who was attempting to cross a stream to get to the next village, where she was to marry her beloved. The stream had grown full and swift from the recent spring rains. There was no way the bride-to-be could cross it without damaging her beautiful gown.

After sizing up the situation, the elderly monk walked over to the bride, picked her up and gently carried her across the roaring water. Then he placed her safe and sound on the other side. The woman thanked him and went on her way to her wedding.

The young monk was angry and astonished. He couldn't believe the man he respected so much had broken one of his vows. "How could you touch her?" he asked.

The elderly monk looked at him and said, "It was the right thing to do."

Months went by, and the new monk avoided the elderly monk. He was so upset and disappointed in his mentor that he refused to speak to him.

Then one night, as the elderly monk was leaving evening prayers, the young monk stopped him in the hallway. "I must ask you again. I cannot stop thinking about it. How could you break your vow and carry the woman across the stream?"

The elder monk replied, "My friend, I carried her but once for a brief moment and let her go. You, on the other hand, seem to have been carrying her for months."

The point, of course, is that it's easy to carry our hurt, anger and disappointment around with us for a long time.

What is the latest hurt you are carrying around? In a few words, write down who hurt you and what happened below and on the next page.

 *Who hurt you and what happened?*

Now write down the names of everyone you have shared what happened to you.

 *The people I have told about what happened:*

Now ask yourself, "How often do I think or talk about what happened?"

 *How often I think about or talk aout what happened:*

Now let's look at your situation. You answered the first question, so you know what happened. You've shared it with some people, which you need to do to start the forgiveness process.

Take a look at the second question: the one with the names of people you told about what happened. If you haven't shared the situation with more than three or four people and aren't thinking or talking about it often, then congratulations: you're probably ready to move on and forgive. Way to go! But, if there are more than three or four names listed, you might be holding onto your hurt feelings and can't let go yet.

Now let's look at the third question: how often you think or talk about what happened. If you're talking or thinking about it a lot, chances are you're stuck in your feelings. That's not good at all.

Part of the problem with holding onto feelings of hurt and resentment is that you can easily end up in the gossip vineyard, telling everyone about how awful it is that someone did something to you. Either that or you may find yourself creating even more drama by sending vicious text messages or leaving comments on people's MySpace pages that slam the person who slammed you. Okay, so you feel a whole lot better because you aired your grudge about the person who did you wrong. But you also hurt a lot of people because you couldn't let it go. What purpose does that serve?

LETTING GO IS GOOD FOR YOUR HEALTH

The other problem with holding onto your negative emotions is that it's bad for you, physically as well as emotionally. Yes, it really is bad for your body.

Remember what we learned in Chapter Four about the physiological effects of jealousy? Feelings of jealousy cause your brain to release stress chemicals that are harmful. Holding onto your grievances is just as harmful: it can raise your blood pressure and increase your heart rate, which puts a strain on your entire system. Not only that, it triggers your limbic system, which in turn releases all sorts of stress chemicals throughout your body—none of which are good for your long-term health. And we've mentioned before, once your limbic system is activated, it prevents you from connecting with your prefrontal cortex, the part of your brain that allows you to make good, healthy decisions. What happens inside whenever you hold onto your hurts really is a chain reaction.

And you know something? The longer you hang onto those feelings of hurt and resentment, the more you set off that chain reaction. The more you set off the chain, the more damage you do to your body. The more you damage your body, the more you decrease your chances for a healthy, happy life.

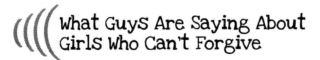

DR. JENN SAYS...

No one dies from too much joy in a lifetime. But people can die from too much anger.

Constantly dwelling over what happened doesn't do you any good. That's why forgiveness is not only a gift to others but a gift you give yourself.

Letting go of your hurt, anger, and resentment means you now have more room in your heart for more positive feelings. And when you cultivate positive feelings, you set off another chain reaction—only this one's *good* for your body! Ultimately, it means you will have more room for healthy emotions that help your body fight off infection, heal, and keep your cardiovascular system in tip-top shape.

To my knowledge, no one can die from too much joy. But we *can* die from too much anger because it stresses out our cardiovascular system.

Remember, guys today have strong feelings about girls who don't know how to forgive. Just read some of their comments below. Then imagine how much more they'll respect and appreciate that you've shown them that you can forgive for good.

What Guys Are Saying About Girls Who Can't Forgive

I think women don't forgive. They are like a rolodex. You may think they will forget, but one day your mistake will pop up again in their brains and they will say, "Remember that?"
  –Alex, USA

The things I have noticed most about forgiveness is it is so easy to say, "I forgive you." But in actuality, you are forgiven until you mess up again, and then that rabbit will be pulled right out of the hat again to haunt you.
    –Dwight, USA

No girl forgives your past mistakes. They will be used against you in every argument for as long as you are with her, whether it was something small or big. It doesn't matter. It is stuck in her head, and it is a stick in her purse that she uses to beat you with, whenever the occasion arises.
    –Storm, USA

With a girl there is no such thing as real forgiveness. I think if they run out of something to hate on you for during an argument, they go back to what you screwed up on, maybe even years ago, and bring that back up again so that they show they have dominance because they're reminding you and thinking: "You're a man, and you're not perfect. Nobody's perfect, but if anybody was, it would be a woman."
    –Kevin, USA

FORGIVE OTHERS
BUT REMEMBER TO FORGIVE YOURSELF

So how do you keep yourself from ruminating over the wrong that someone did to you? The same way you keep your IBSC in check. Whenever you find yourself replaying the memories of what happened or wanting to share your story with someone for the forty-millionth time, go into movie mode. Put your mind in neutral, and watch yourself having the thought or the desire to go tell the world what happened. Eventually, the desire to dwell on it or tell someone about it will lessen and lessen and lessen. Once you commit to letting go of the hurt, you're ready to forgive.

There are other ways to help you let go of your negative feelings. Here's how one girl did it. For reasons of privacy, she asked me not to give her name. But I can tell you this: her story is so powerful, it practically speaks for itself:

> *I once fell in love with this great guy. Oh, my God, he was the most wonderful guy in the whole world. I mean, he was the one. I wanted to marry him.*
>
> *But after dating a few months, I got pregnant, and he ditched me—just like that! I went to the clinic all by myself and terminated the pregnancy. He didn't bother to show up. I couldn't believe it! God, how I hated him.*
>
> *I cried myself to sleep every night. I would drive by his house and shout "Fuck you!" hoping he could hear me. I wrote him nasty messages. I did everything I knew to make him miserable. I wanted him to pay for what he had done to me. All I could think about was how I could pay him back for being such an asshole.*
>
> *I thought about it every day. It took over so much of my thinking that I lost weight and couldn't focus in classes. All I could think about was how he had done something awful to me. I wanted him to die.*
>
> *That was the moment that made me stop and realize I was losing it. I was making myself sick with resentment. He didn't seem to be suffering—I was. He wasn't losing weight, and doing terrible in class—I was.*
>
> *My mom didn't know what had happened, but she knew I was having trouble. So she sent me to a therapist. That didn't help much, although it did give me a chance to talk about my feelings.*
>
> *I decided to try to forgive my ex ... just a little. But just when I thought I had forgiven him, something would remind me of how badly he hurt me, and I would get angry again. How was I supposed to let go so I could get back to my life?*
>
> *One day I got the courage to call him up and ask if we could talk. We met over lunch. I told him I was pissed off and having a hard time with everything. He said he was sorry. He*

told me he got scared when he found out I was pregnant. He didn't know what to do, so he dropped me. He was afraid his foster mom would kick him out of the house. He didn't know where to turn.

I had no idea he was so scared of losing his foster family. But that made sense, as he had already been bounced around several times before.

After I left lunch, I thought a lot about his side of the story. It helped some to realize why he had treated me like he did.

But still ... I found it hard to let go! I still needed him to know how badly he had hurt me. I still wanted him to pay somehow.

One morning, I woke up to the first snow of the season. It was so beautiful. It was a Saturday, no school. I sat by the window and watched the snow falling for the longest time when suddenly something changed in my heart. I realized that I was part of this bigger thing than just my simple little life. Seasons were changing. Life was moving on, doing what it does. I was stuck in my anger and resentment and wasn't moving forward. Life was passing me by, because I was stuck on something that had happened months ago.

I got out my journal and wrote a long letter to my ex. Then I wrote a letter to my baby, whose life I ended, and apologized. I realized that I was asking my baby to forgive me—just like my boyfriend had asked me to forgive him.

I decided to really let my hate go. It wasn't serving anyone. And I want to be a good person, you know? I want to be of help to others. I want a good life. So I made a deal with myself. Every time I felt hate or anger toward my ex, I promised myself I would remind myself that he is human, and he made a mistake. Hell, I have made mistakes, too—some big ones even.

It's not always easy ... but every day it's better. What I find helps the most is to stop myself when I begin to ruminate over it. I remember the peace I felt looking out on the quiet dance of winter's first snowfall. I replace my anger with that peace.

The girl in this story used nature to help her replace her anger and hurt so she could forgive. She acknowledged it isn't always easy. Forgiveness isn't always easy. But at least she is trying her best. That's all anyone can ask of oneself.

This powerful story reminds us of two important facets of forgiveness. The first one, we've already touched on: none of us is perfect. All of us *need* forgiveness.

Secondly, all of us are *worthy* of forgiveness. And that, my friends, is really the key.

You are worthy of forgiveness. You cant love others until you forgive yourself for your shortcomings and mistakes.

Take a few minutes to think of the things that you want to forgive yourself for. Put your hands over your heart, breathe deeply, and allow yourself to feel love for *your entire self*—even the parts of you that may not be perfect, even the times when you screwed up so badly you still can't quite believe it. Write down your thoughts below.

 *I Forgive Myself For:*

Remember, unless you can let go of those feelings of guilt and learn to forgive yourself, all those destructive feelings that hurt your body and drive you to hurt others will only continue to fester.

To love someone means you embrace all of them, the light and the dark. Embrace your own darkness and show it some compassion by offering yourself the gift of forgiveness.

SLOW DOWN AND BREATHE

Even in today's fast-paced, high-speed world of instant-access technology, sometimes it's still the old-fashioned things—like stopping to look at nature—that keep us centered and calm. Like the girl in the story, you can also use a peaceful image of nature or anything else that soothes you to quiet your negative feelings or memories of people who've wronged you.

Here's how to do that:

What part of nature do you love the most? Or is it music or dancing that you love, that brings you peace?

Take a moment to think about your favorite parts of what you love and how it makes you calm. Maybe you are visualizing a snowstorm. Or maybe it's the sound of your favorite song. Feels good all over, doesn't it?

Now that you've stretched the muscles of your imagination, let's try this breathing and visualization exercise that can also help you move toward forgiveness. It's adapted from a breathing practice found in the book *Forgive for Good* by Dr. Fred Luskin, a psychologist who is among the leaders in research on forgiveness. (You may want to read the entire instructions first before you do this.)

1. First, think of the event that got your hackles up. Use the one you wrote about a few pages ago if you like. Play the event over in your mind so you remember everything that upset you. Take a moment to check in with how it feels in your body. On a scale of 1–10, how upset are you? Write that number down here _____.

2. Now think about the place or thing that makes you peaceful. Close your eyes and visualize that thing or place.
3. Next, take deep, slow breaths. Close your eyes. Inhale to the count of seven, exhale to the count of eleven. (This is known as 7–11 breathing.) Place your hands over your heart and hold the image of what makes you peaceful over your heart. When you have done five to ten deep breaths, slowly open your eyes.
4. Now think about the event that upset you. On a scale of 1–10, how upset are you? Write your number here _____. If you are like most people, you will find a significant decrease in how upset you are.

Our culture today, with all its technology and fast-paced life, encourages a frantic, rat-race mentality that leads to great accomplishments but also frazzled nerves. If you slow down, unplug, and close your eyes and focus on something that calms you, chances are, the thing that made you angry or upset will slowly fade away.

Breathing and visualizing also keep us from triggering the mechanisms in our brain that bring on anger and stress. When you can lessen your hurt feelings and calm yourself down, you know you can forgive and forget.

IT'S GOOD TO FORGIVE AND FORGET

Remember, if you can't forgive and let go, your Dream Girl crown can easily slip off. That's exactly what happened to Christina, another Dream Girl-in-training. Christina met Mike at the start of their junior year in high school, and the pair quickly began dating. They were a happy couple and didn't fight a lot. Then right before their senior year began, a new girl moved into the neighborhood. Mike started hanging out with the new girl in between some classes. Christina got worried that Mike was spending too much time with her.

Right before Thanksgiving break, someone started gossiping that Mike had cheated on Christina with the new girl. Christina was devastated. When she confronted Mike about the new girl, he confessed he had been at a party, and he had indeed hooked up with her. He felt terribly ashamed and asked Christina to forgive him. But she said no way. She dropped him on the spot.

Christina began dating all types of guys and having sex with them just to get back at Mike. She didn't really like any of the guys she had sex with, but that didn't matter. All that mattered was getting revenge on Mike.

Before too long ... you guessed it. Christina ended up with a bad reputation. Guys who just wanted sex knew they could score with her, so her phone rang off the hook. As far as everyone at school was concerned, she was just another just-in-his-jeans girl.

It took almost a year and an STD before Christina realized she was only hurting herself by not forgiving and forgetting. Once she forgave Mike and let the hurt go, she zipped up her pants and stopped handing herself out like trick-or-treat candy to every guy who wanted a piece of her. It took a while for her to mend her reputation, but eventually she did.

Once Christina cleaned up her act and learned to forget about the past, so did everyone else at school.

Another girl shared this story:

I hated a girl I'll call Betsy. I felt Betsy stole my boyfriend from me. I blasted her on MySpace and sent her text messages every day telling her what a whore she was. I told everyone what Betsy had done to me. After a few months, I noticed that my friends weren't calling me as much anymore to hang out. I normally got a zillion text messages every day, and then I hardly got any at all.

I asked one of my good friends what was up with that. She didn't seem to want to talk to me about it. I could tell something was up. I kept asking her until she finally gave in and confessed that people were tired of hearing me always complain about what Betsy had done to me. My friends felt like I couldn't hear anything they had to share about themselves, as I was so preoccupied with what had happened to me. My staying angry and being in the victim role turned off my friends.

I was embarrassed to hear the truth but glad that my friend told me.

I knew the only way to get on with my life was to forgive Betsy. I went over to where she worked one day, and when she went on her break, I asked if I could hang out with her. She was totally surprised and I think a bit scared. I told her I was sorry about the way I had handled everything and that I wanted to let it all go. She looked so relieved. I knew she was still with my ex, but it didn't seem to matter anymore. They were happy together.

Betsy and I aren't friends, but at least I stopped being such a bitch, and in my heart it feels better to let go of my anger.

Letting go of our hurt and learning to forgive doesn't mean we have to become best friends with the person who hurt us. There will always be people who you don't care to hang out with and that's perfectly okay.

Bonus Secret

Life can be messy sometimes, and there are times when we are angry. It's when we let our anger block our path to the future that we need to stop, breathe, let go and forgive.

What isn't okay is when we hold a grudge and make ourselves and others miserable. That not only pushes people away, it pushes you closer to looking like a just-in-his-jeans girl.

Life can get messy fast—so fast sometimes that we don't know what it hit us. Friends get hurt. Girls get assaulted and raped. People die. None of us like it when bad things happen, especially to people we know and love. There are times when we need to feel anger, sadness, or grief. But life goes on. There comes a time when we must let go of our sadness and move on.

Please, do not think that I am minimizing the horror of what can happen in this world or that all you need to do is to stop and breathe for everything to go away. Some events are so traumatic that you may need to seek professional help to work through your feelings of pain. And some pains last longer than others.

What I am saying is that, in most cases—for the kinds of hurt that we all deal with every day on the road to life and love—by following the steps to forgiveness, your life will be fuller and your capacity for compassion greater, and your ability to attract people in all the ways that matter will remain a cut above. That's what Dream Girls strive for.

What Guys Are Saying About Girls Who Know How to Forgive

I am with a wonderful woman who knows how to forgive. She should have dumped me when we first met because I screwed up, but she didn't. I am so thankful she forgave me and moved on. We have a wonderful relationship because of her.
    –Mike, USA

Being forgiven takes such a load off of your shoulders. It's like I feel I can breathe again. I don't like it when I know I have hurt someone and they stay pissed off at me.
    –Jon, USA

A girl who knows how to forgive and never throws your shit back in your face is a rare thing. I would love to find a girl who can do that. Hopefully, I can do the same for her.
    –Chris, USA

Forgiving is one of the best gifts you can give to others. Guys respect girls who know how to forgive and move on with their lives. Holding onto your anger or hurt isn't attractive in the long run. Your compassion for others is what makes you truly gorgeous.

Here is the difference between a Dream Girl and a just-in-his-jeans girl when it comes to forgiveness. See how you measure up. If you need to work on letting go of past hurts, try using movie mode or the breathing exercise you learned to help you move back into the present moment and into a happier, brighter future.

DREAM GIRLS	JUST-IN-HIS-JEANS GIRLS
• Don't hold onto anger	• Hold onto anger
• Understand that people make mistakes	• Can't imagine how anyone could ever do something wrong to them
• Are aware of the times they have hurt others	• Can't see their own mistakes or the hurt they have caused
• Know that forgiveness is a sign of health	• Could care less if their anger is eating away at them and hurting their body and soul
• Do not drudge up old mistakes	• Throw old mistakes in peoples' faces every chance they get
• See no need to seek revenge or paybacks	• Want to hurt those who have hurt them

Now that you have added the forgiveness jewel to your Dream Girl crown, you're almost ready to shine. I say *almost* because even Dream Girls can say things or do things that drive a guy crazy. In the final chapter, we're going to learn about some of the things that guys today wish girls would stop doing, so that your crown will absolutely sparkle. Grab your highlighter; there may be one or two (or more) things that hit home.

"Knock That Off!" The Things Guys Wish You'd Stop Doing

"There are some great girls out there, but they do some really stupid things that make guys lose respect for them or not take them seriously or just annoy them. Dr. Jenn, can't you tell them to "Knock that shit off?"
–Russell, USA

Russell makes a good point, girls. There is so much to think about on your way to becoming a Dream Girl—so many secrets to remember and potholes that can throw you off balance—that even the best, most well-intentioned girl is liable to mess up once in a while.

Then again, who said you have to be perfect?

Remember, a Dream Girl is by no means a "perfect girl," because no such thing exists. She is, however, a well-rounded human being with good values, good judgment, and compassion. She listens to others and treats them with respect. She *shows* love in action, even if she isn't *feeling* it, because that's how *she* wants to be treated. She knows how to forgive. She knows she'll make mistakes, but when that happens, she doesn't let it overwhelm her. Rather, she tries to learn from her mistakes because she knows they can help her grow into the kind of person who can one day sustain a happy, healthy, long-lasting relationship with some very special guy.

In other words, she strives every day to be her best. That's all anyone can expect.

Still, because nobody's perfect, even a would-be Dream Girl has moments when she says things or does things—whether she means to or not—that can drive a guy absolutely crazy.

What about you? What are some of the behaviors or habits that can make you seem less than a Dream Girl? Be honest; every one of us has at least one area in our lives that we can improve upon.

Our friends can help us when we want to improve ourselves. Every one of us has a friend or circle of friends whom we can turn to whenever we need help. That's why I created that sort of environment on my MySpace site, located at myspace.com/jenniferaustinleigh. It's a place where lots of people—people from all over the world—write to me about what isn't working in their lives or post comments, asking others for help or feedback. I also created a Facebook profile, so I can reach the users of that VSN.

I feel very privileged that so many of you—girls and guys alike—appreciate my sites because you know they are a place where you can be yourself and sound off about what's on your mind. And when it comes to talking about the things they wish girls knew, the guys have been refreshingly honest ... and insightful.

This last chapter shares some of the opinions, observations, and heartfelt requests from guys aged fifteen to twenty-one from all around the world. I asked them to talk about the things they'd like you to stop doing, in order to earn their respect and affection—you know, the things that can make you a Dream Girl, instead of a just-in-his-jeans girl.

If you have ever wished you could be a fly on the wall and listen in when guys are venting about girls, you'll find this chapter particularly enlightening. Some of their answers might even surprise you.

I want girls to stop assuming guys know that they have feelings for us. I would like it if girls would just be as up-front with their emotions as they expect guys to be.
   –Kyle, USA

Ladies, stop lowering yourself to [being] an object of desire. Keep your pride and dignity; don't intentionally be a target of lust. It will only hurt you in the long run.
   –Dusty, USA

Stop flirting with guys when you have a boyfriend.
   –Travis, USA

Stop going for the guys who are assholes. Go for the guys who treat you well. You will be happier in the long run as opposed to being with the "bad boy."
   –J. J., USA

Don't think all guys are the same. A guy will like a girl and want to be with her, and the girl will say "I've heard that before," and that kills it right there. Girls think they have you all figured out before they get to know you. It's disrespectful.
   –Woody, USA

Stop pestering your boyfriend[s] about cheating if you know they aren't. It makes you a nag. If you think they are cheating, you shouldn't be with them.
   –Edmund, England

Stop trying to change someone to be what you want them to be.
   –Dale, USA

Don't beat around the bush and hide your emotions and be a bitch. If you want a relationship to work, you have to work

through problems. If you go around them, it's a lot of bullshit to deal with later.
    –Chris, USA

Stop being so hard on yourselves, like calling yourself fat or ugly. Guys don't like it, especially when it gets excessive.
    –Erik, USA

Stop nagging. Guys hate it!
    –Marvin, USA

Stop buying guys' lies. Don't do things just because a guy says those three magic words, "I love you." If you are dying that much for love, then please find something real. The guy who has been slamming back beers for the past several hours and can barely slur out a sentence is not going to be your prince charming. Don't sell your hearts so quickly. Don't do anything you are uncomfortable with.
    –Taj, USA

Please stop talking loud when you are with your little group of friends when you're at a party. I realize this is a method of drawing attention to yourself, but I am not a shark that comes swimming around when I smell chum in the water. If you want to talk to someone, go talk to them; otherwise I'll just be annoyed that my conversation is being interrupted by your irrelevant, loud chatter.
    –Graham, England

Stop complaining when you are in a bad relationship when you are with the guy just because he is a rebel or cool. You chose to be with the bad boy!
    –Clark, USA

Stop dressing so slutty! The girls wonder why they are called sluts and hos when they are dressed as one. Duh!
   –Tony, USA

Please open up and show guys your feelings. We hate it when a girl can't say what's on her mind or share her feelings.
   –Mike, USA

Please don't think we are mind readers and we should always know what you are feeling, or that we should know what you think we did wrong. If you are mad at a guy, tell him. Don't just pout and give him the silent treatment. How are we supposed to make it better if we don't know what we did in the first place? Learn to forgive.
   –Kenny, USA

Please don't tell me about "Joe Blow" down the street and how he does this or that better. I am who I am; deal with it. I can't change for you.
   –Jonathan, USA

Don't be a know-it-all. Allow me to have an opinion without you trying to better it all the time. Listen to me. Show me some respect by hearing and understanding what I have to say.
   –Jessie, USA

Don't give in to sex so quickly. Guys like the hunt. If you allow them to sleep with you right away, they will lose interest and not call you the next day. Sex doesn't build a relationship, ladies.
   –Robert, England

Stop being so damn stubborn! Try to be a little more understanding, please.
   –Jake, USA

Stop worrying about how you look or how "big" you look. If we are talking to you and interested in you to date, we probably love the way you look.
    –Brian, USA

Develop a good judge of character and stop seeking out the guys who believe women are objects and only want them as possessions and all that other clichéd but true stuff.
    –John, USA

You don't have to use your bodies to get what you want in life. I have met a lot of girls who use their bodies or their orifices to get a guy to love them or to get what they want from a guy.
    –James, USA

Don't make everything so dramatic! You only end up getting yourself frustrated over things that really don't matter much to begin with.
    –Brent, USA

Please stop taking guys to the mall to shop. After an hour, it gets annoying, and it's worse if you don't thank him for it. Most guys do not like to go shopping. Please say, "Thank you for going with me." Show that you value our efforts.
    –Mike, USA

You can't be a bitch and expect me to respect you when you don't respect me.
    –Brandon, USA

I hate drama. Stop it!
    –Cody, USA

You are not your boyfriend's mother. Stop being so controlling.
    –Sheriff, USA

A guy can only take so much of you hitting him in the arm when you make a joke or want his attention. After awhile, it gets irritating as hell.

   –Bryan, USA

I generally believe in body art, but if you get a tattoo, you have to be willing to live with it for the rest of your life. If a girl gets a tattoo on a private area of her body, that tells me she expects people to see it. How does that make me respect her?

   –Joshua, USA

Don't be fake. Be who you are. If you have problems, tell them to your boyfriend. Don't try to be someone you aren't.

   –Eddie, USA

I wish girls would stop talking shit about each other. They compare each other and are mean. It's like they hate other girls. It's not attractive.

   –Julio, USA

When girls use sex to get love, it doesn't work. Stop it.

   –Shane, USA

One of the most destructive things a girl can do is to talk about her sexual relationship with her boyfriend to her friends. Most girls aren't aware of how bad this is.

   –Aladdin, USA

Girls who put themselves down in order to get a compliment drive me crazy! What am I supposed to say to them? It pisses me off. They are either fishing for a compliment or terribly insecure. Either way, it's a turnoff!

   –Russell, USA

If a guy has a female friend he has known longer than his new

girlfriend, and there is no sexual attraction with the friend, the girlfriend shouldn't make the guy choose between her and the old friend. I'll choose my old friend because I have known her longest, and the new girlfriend might not last. Don't make us make choices. Know we have platonic friends before you came into the picture. Deal with it!
    –Kyle, USA

I wish girls were more relaxed and had a more happy-go-lucky attitude.
    –Robert, USA

Don't lie. There is nothing more unattractive. Nothing is more beautiful than a girl who can tell a guy the truth.
    –Bede, England

Stop appearing so self-confident if you aren't. Trying to be posh all by yourself is stupid.
    –Antoine, France

Stop gossiping and bad-mouthing people. I've lost count of the amount of times I've had girls tell me stuff about other people. If that person wanted me to know that stuff, then they would have told me, right?
    –Jason, USA

Girls who claim to be high maintenance drive me crazy. Seriously, knock that shit off. It takes two people to make a relationship work. If you think you are worth more attention than your partner, you aren't worth his time!
    –Sam, New Zealand

Don't pull out an old conversation or an argument from a week ago, whether we settled it or not. Just drop it!
    –Ariki, New Zealand

Stop taking everything so personally. Just because I have had a bad day doesn't mean you have been the cause. Let me have my space and, when I am ready to talk, I will. Paranoia is not attractive.
   –Paul, USA

Girls, stop checking up on us all the time. It's annoying.
   –Gary, Ireland

Stop being promiscuous or going to sex parties. You can cover it up, but it doesn't make you less dirty.
   –Matt, USA

Don't be too fast with the sexual things. Everyone needs time, including men, to figure it all out.
   –Dirk, Germany

If you let me hook up with you right away, I lose respect for you.
   –Tony, USA

Please don't be so arrogant!
   –Faut, Germany

Stop playing games. If I like you, then try to believe me. Don't try to get my attention by threatening to kill yourself or cutting yourself. I don't need that. It's impossible to love a girl who damages her own body just to get noticed. I have known enough of these kinds of girls that now I look for old scars because I can't handle it anymore.
   –Avrom, New Zealand

Can't girls value the love they have been given?
   –Gary, USA

Stop complaining about your weight. Work out or shut up! I know that sounds mean, but seriously, though. It's easy enough to change. Complaining won't get my sympathy.
   –Tariq, Brazil

Don't say, "It's me, not you." Don't play that game. We can handle the truth.
   –Waylon, Antarctica

Don't expect us to pay for everything!
   –Zaki, Algeria

Stop being bitchy, stuck up, and acting like every man is a pig. Not all of us are.
   –Fragiskos, Greece

Stop worrying so much about how you look for your boyfriend. He obviously is attracted to you. He isn't going to forget the girl he can't stop thinking about if you take five minutes less to finish your makeup.
   –Neil, Canada

Stop doubting us when we tell you that you're beautiful. That doubt is what makes you ugly.
   –Andrew, USA

Don't cheat on your boyfriend, especially if you have cheated in the past and he took you back and forgave you. You can damage a guy for life.
   –Erik, USA

You might technically be a virgin if you have not had intercourse, but if you are giving head, you aren't a virgin in my eyes. Stop claiming to be so innocent. You aren't.
   –Roberto, Mexico

Don't take too many drugs. It's not pretty.
    –Ashwin, England

Stop dating the assholes. When you do this, then you'll stop thinking we are all assholes and learn a little more from your dating experiences. Find the shy kid, and you will learn how much of the world he will try to give you.
    –Kyle, USA

One thing I don't like is when girls complain to me all the time. Sure, I'm an understanding guy, but I can't listen to that shit all the time.
    –Josh, USA

Stop reading between the lines. If I say something, it does not mean that I mean something else.
    –Shaun, South Africa

If your boyfriend says you're beautiful, don't argue! It annoys us.
    –Jacob, USA

Don't emotionally bitch slap me in public.
    –Stewart, USA

Don't be disrespectful to your body. It is so precious.
    –Kash, USA

Don't be jealous of a guy's friends. If there is no sexual attraction, then be confident in your own relationship with him. Guys need to keep their friends from before they met you.
    –Robert, USA

Don't act like our mothers. Don't try to mother us up—treat us like your boyfriend.
    –Ace, USA

Don't be fake. If you don't like something then tell me, and don't pretend like you're enjoying it when you're really not— because then I am wasting my time and yours.
   –Janek, USA

I want girls to stop using their vaginas to gain power.
   –Shannon, USA

Girls need to stop lying! Girls are really bad at lying.
   –Kundell, Tonga

Girls need to stop leading men on. Some girls do it as a sport or something, just to see if the guy will go for it.
   –Caleb, USA

Girls, stop looking for love when you are already in a relationship with someone. There's no need to be looking for someone better when you are still with someone else. Girls should value the love given to them because you never know if you will ever find another person that will love you deeply.
   –Jonathan, Philippines

Stop playing games.
   –Ike, Congo

I want girls to stop thinking so much about what a guy said, like a week ago.
   –Sergio, Costa Rica

Learn to listen better. I can't stand it when a girl can't hear what I have to say.
   –John, USA

Turn off your cell phone when you are with me. Stop texting and trying to listen to me at the same time.
   –Lewis, USA

If you are mad at me, let me know before you attack me on my profile. I don't need your shitty comments posted for everyone to read. That's so immature.
–Jesse, USA

Now that you've heard what these guys want you to know, ask yourself: How many times did they talk about things that I can improve on? How many of their messages surprised me? Which one (or ones) got my attention the most?

Did you read all of their comments, or did you speed past some?

If you did skip past some of them, then I want you to slow down, hit the brakes, reread the messages, and take them all in. Highlight or underline the ones that you feel like you need to work on.

Here's a fun way to have a "self talk" about things that the guys quotes make you want to work on. Grab a piece of paper and, with the hand you normally write with, write down questions for yourself, like, "What do I need to do to stop ...?" or "What makes me ...?" You get the idea. Write any question you want. Then switch your pen or pencil to your non-dominant hand—obviously, the one you don't normally write with—and answer those questions.

It's especially interesting to do this with a big sheet of paper and a crayon. Why? Because unless you happen to be ambidextrous, all the wisdom you have about yourself—you know, *before* your Itty Bitty Shitty Committee kicked in—will voice its opinion when you write with your non-dominant hand.

You handwriting will probably be a bit wobbly. Don't worry about that. We use our brains differently when we write with the hand we normally don't use. That's what makes the truth easier to be revealed.

A word of caution: This exercise can tap into some really deep emotions. If something comes up that you need to talk to someone about, call a friend or message me at MySpace or Facebook or send me a line at jennifer@drjennforgirls.com.

Remember, guys want you to become a Dream Girl. *They really do.* Girls who develop a healthy sense of self-respect get respected. If you really work the exercises in this book and read and absorb what guys have to say, you are well on your way to becoming a Dream Girl.

what guys want you to know:

Guys want you to know lots of things. Listen to what they have to say. Their comments are the road signs to help you get to Dream Girl-dom and keep you from being a just-in-his-jeans-girl.

Secret No. 38

DR. JENN'S PAJAMA PARTY

You've come a long way, haven't you? Now that you have your Dream Girl crown with all its sparkling jewels, you've never been so attractive. But we all know that learning new things takes practice. Now that you're done with the book, it's important to remember what you have learned along the way, as you continue your journey through life and love.

One way to keep your focus on being a Dream Girl and share what you've learned is to have what I call a Dr. Jenn's Pajama Party. Invite your best friends over and spend time talking about the things that can help each one of you remain a Dream Girl. It takes a lot of support these days to keep your Dream Girl tiara shining.

"You're funny, Dr. Jenn. *A pajama party?* I haven't had a "sleepover" since I was, well, a long time ago. Those are for little girls."

Now I realize most of you are at an age where you've been hanging with your friends and talking about girl stuff for awhile, so it can be hard to remember how exciting it was the first time your mom let you have a few friends stay over on a Friday night and stay up past your bedtime. And even if you *do* remember, you probably think, "Oh, that is *so* kid stuff."

Maybe you're right. Then again, sometimes it's the simple things, like hanging out in your pj's late at night with your closest friends just like when you were younger, that bring us the most joy. I'm just saying, give it a try and see for yourself.

Keep me posted about how you are doing with your new Dream Girl crown or about the new jewels you have discovered that help make you shine.

Or write me if you are having any problems. I'll do my best to stay in touch. I'll be posting lots of info on my blog at MySpace: www.myspace.com/jenniferaustinleigh and on my website, www.drjennforgirls.com. Or you can email me at jennifer@drjennforgirls.com.

I wish you all the very best in becoming a Dream Girl.

All the best!
Dr. Jenn

THE SECRETS

1. Guys like girls with self-respect. Knowing that is the first step on the road to becoming a Dream Girl.

2. It's really hard if your negative self-thoughts overrule anything nice that we have to say about you. What guys want you to know

3. Girls who invite guys to see their best get the most respect.

4. Guys are attracted to the energy that comes from a girl with self-respect.

5. Guys don't like being disrespected any more than you do. Dream Girls know that showing a guy simple respect goes a long way to helping him attain what he needs to grow and thrive.

6. Girls who know how to listen well will have more meaningful relationships.

7. Guys have respect for girls who know how to be "detective listeners.

8. Your sincere desire to learn more about a guy says more about you than any words that come out of your mouth.

9. Hijacking a conversation is not cool.

10. Guys think girls who are posers are positively annoying.

11. Guys wish girls would stop worrying about themselves and pay more attention to them.

12. Guys want girls to explore the meaning of the things they say.

13. Guys want you to know that they need to be sure they can trust you—today, and every day.

14. Guys want girls to play fair. No Cheating!

15. Many guys consider "cyber flirting" to be a form of cheating.

16. Guys want to know what's true for you so that you can be true to yourself and to them.

17. Guys want you to know that even though it's stressful, it's always better to tell the truth.

18. Jacking a password is a major show of disrespect.

19. Guys don't want you to ignore their messages or them.

20. Guys want girls to use electronic communication respectfully.

21. Guys don't value girls who take pleasure in the pain of others.

22. Guys don't respect or trust girls who gossip because gossiping is not love in action. Guys show more love and respect to girls who know how to show love and respect.

23. Guys don't like it when you and your friends gossip about other people. They want you to find healthier ways to feel connected.

24. Guys don't appreciate girls who diss on their friends or family. They especially hate it when girls diss on themselves.

25. Guys want you to take responsibility for your nagging and stop making excuses for it.

26. Guys don't like girls who get jealous too easily.

27. Guys are drawn to the inner beauty that self-confidence provides.

28. Being confident does not mean being perfect. Guys want you to know that your best is always good enough, so long as you continue to try.

29. Guys are tired of seeing so much skin.

30. Guys want you to know that girls who are too into alcohol or drugs aren't what they are looking for in a romantic partner.

31. Guys don't kneel at the feet of drama queens. Instead, they run from them ... as fast as they possibly can!

32. Guys like girls who let their accomplishments and good qualities speak for themselves, rather than drawing attention to themselves or their qualities.

33. Guys today feel that girls have become way too sexually aggressive. Deep down, guys wish that girls would go back to acting like ladies. That's because deep down, guys would like to go back to being gentlemen.

34. Guys like fast cars. They don't like fast girls.

35. Guys like girls who don't pressure them for sex.

36. Dream Girls respect virginity, whether it is their virginity or his. They don't give it away, and they don't take it away casually. They know and respect that the heart has a say in the matter. They listen for what the heart has to say.

37. Guys want you to learn how to forgive.

38. Guys want you to know lots of things. Listen to what they have to say. Their comments are the road signs to help you get to Dream Girl-dom and keep you from being a just-in-his-jeans-girl.

ABOUT DR. JENN

Jennifer Austin Leigh, PsyD. is a life coach for teen girls and their mothers. She is passionate about helping teen girls find their way in today's turbulent tide of technological and cultural changes, and helping moms deal with the emotional roller coaster of parenting a teen.

She works with families across the United States.

Dr. Jenn, as her readers and clients know her, speaks about love and respect to girls in middle school and high school at their schools. She also speaks to mothers of teen girls to help them understand "growing up girl" in today's world. She hosts Dr. Jenn Pajama Parties for teen girls around the world.

Her four children, John, Natalie, Louis and William, are her greatest inspiration. She is currently working on her third book, "Mom, You Just Don't Get It!" Dr. Jenn lives in San Francisco, California.

www.drjennforgirls.com

 DREAM GIRL JEWELS

Think of every piece of information you learn about yourself as you grow and change towards becoming a Dream Girl as a jewel that fits perfectly in your Dream Girl crown. On these next few pages, write down the new jewels you have discovered about yourself and your life. Use these pages as your private Dream Girl Journal.

 If you want to share any of your jewels with me, please email me at jennifer@drjennforgirls.com. I may not be able to answer you, but I will do my best to read all you want to share. I'll hold your shared thoughts with the utmost respect, for after all, that is what we Dream Girls do!

 *These are the jewels I have learned:*

DREAM GIRL JEWELS

DREAM GIRL JEWELS

DREAM GIRL JEWELS

DREAM GIRL JEWELS

DREAM GIRL JEWELS